Dedication

For Jasmine

Flora Macdonald Dempster

HELP ME MUM

AUSTIN MACAULEY
PUBLISHERS LTD.

A CIP catalogue record for this title is available from the British Library.

ISBN 978 1 78455 621 1 (Paperback)
978 1 78455 623 5 (Hardback)

www.austinmacauley.com

First Published (2015)
Austin Macauley Publishers Ltd.
25 Canada Square
Canary Wharf
London
E14 5LB

Printed and bound in Great Britain

Acknowledgments

<ins>My mother,</ins>
<ins>Flora Macdonald.</ins>

You brought my brother Norman and myself up by yourself.
You put food on the table and gave us love and a massive work ethic.
Your motto would be 'make your own way in life.'
I still miss you.

<ins>Ewen A. Cameron,</ins>
<ins>Glen Nevis Estate</ins>
<ins>Fort William</ins>

You at first said don't put yourself through this.
Not only did you read the finished manuscript but you also went to the trouble of proof-reading and correcting without being asked.
A busy man with a multi-million pound business to run and a great personal friend of mine.
Heartfelt thanks xx

<ins>Andrew Murchison</ins>
<ins>Murchison Law</ins>

My thanks for standing by me and enduring the long legal dilemmas against me on swinging over my croft in my favour.
Eight years was a long time but your legal brain won through in the end.
You left me with a lighter heart and a much lighter pocket, but it was well worth it.
Thank you!

<u>Don Evans</u>

What would Morag and I have done without you.
A qualified doctor, a senior social worker in fostering and adoption, as Morag said you did more than her father but you had life experiences both on your own and with clients.
What a shame people like you leave the social work department. Inexperience does more harm than good in social work.
Belford Prince proved you are no Frankie Deettori.
I sometimes wonder how you coped with my varied life.
My love and thanks.

<u>My attorney in Texas.</u>
<u>Randy Berry</u>

A real gentleman, professional and thoughtful.
You never doubted Morag did the right thing by going on the run to San Diego. As you said, the Texas courts left her no other choice.
You loved my daughter and she also loved you.
Life can be so cruel sometimes; you both lost out on happiness.

PROLOGUE

This book is for Jasmine.

It tells the tale of my life, its ups and downs, relationships and, more importantly, the one thing that bonds family units, love.

My story is complex, but yet it is simple. I have had to endure court battles against my only son; I have had to fight against a former partner to keep my croft; and I have had to go through a traumatic custody case in the US. Most of this book focuses on the latter, the case in America and the aftermath of the decision. However, although my story is complex, the one simple thing that comes to the fore in all of this is love. When love between a mother and child is strong, all other things can often pale into insignificance.

Throughout this book I have referred to my daughter as Morag. Born in England in 1964, Morag Dodds was the name given to her. However, when she was in her 20s, Morag decided to change her name to Sarah. Therefore, many people will remember her as Sarah Dodds rather than Morag. But, for clarity, I have referred to her as Morag throughout this book.

When all else fails, just remember, love is stronger than life itself.

WAITING FOR THE VERDICT IN AUSTIN

Austin, located in the American Southwest, is the capital city of Texas. Positioned on the Colorado River, the picturesque city has an interesting history. Mexicans established forts in the area during the early part of the 19th century and their population grew steadily. However, in 1835, Native Americans fought and won battles that eventually resulted in independence from Mexico. Texas became its own independent country with its own president, congress and monetary system.

In 1839, the Texas Congress formed a commission to find a new capital for their country. Vice President Mirabeau B Lamar advised the commissioners to investigate the area that had previously been named Waterloo, principally because of the hills, waterways and scenic surroundings. The city was re-named Austin, in honour of Stephen F Austin, the "Father of Texas" and the Republic's first Secretary of State.

Austin grew steadily in population particularly after a series of battles between the Texas Rangers and the Comanche Indians. The tribe was pushed westward, finally ending the conflicts between the Texans and the Native tribes. However, all was not plain sailing for the governors of Austin. Sam Houston, a politician from further south, teamed up with the Mexican army to attempt to remove the seat of Texas power from Austin to the much preferred town of Houston, about 160 miles eastwards. Sam Houston considered that the capital city of Texas should not be located in such a remote wilderness. Attempts by Houston failed and it was decreed by Congress in 1845 to keep Austin as the capital of the country.

Although this lovely city has a great culture and an interesting history of conflict and victory over those who attempted to take control of it, my reason for being in Austin was for a very different battle. In fact, one could say my battle was very much a modern-day fight. Sitting in our tiny apartment in Red River Street, I thought how far this was from our home in Forres, Scotland.

A music lover's paradise, the Red River District of Austin is well known for live music venues. Apparently, it is possible to see more than twenty bands playing live gigs in a three-block area. Austin's official slogan is the Live Music Capital of the World, with more music venues per capita than anywhere else in the US.

As the bands played outside, and as people went about their daily lives, Morag, my lovely daughter, and I sat looking at each other, waiting, and willing, for the phone to ring.

It was Thursday 23 February 1995.

Morag busied herself with some dishwashing. I tried to tidy up the apartment but I really couldn't concentrate on domestic chores. A few hours ago, I had been sitting in Supreme Court 32 of the Travis County Courthouse in downtown Austin, listening to the closing arguments skilfully presented by our attorney, Terry Weeks.

Terry was a nice man. A very competent practising attorney in Austin, he had taken on Morag's case after hearing about her plight in the local media. Although he had handled many divorces and custody squabbles he was fascinated by this young woman who had risked so much for the love of her child. As I looked across at my beautiful daughter in that tiny apartment on a February day, I too was struck by her courage. Maybe Morag was doing what every mother of a small child would do – fight to get her offspring back. However, I thought Morag was anything but the usual mother. She had courage, she went to jail to fight for her child and she had just endured a six-day trial in a foreign country to show that she could legitimately care for her daughter, Jasmine. As much as I believed in my daughter, the wait in that apartment was unbearable.

Terry had been impressed by Morag, and Morag took well to him too. Morag was in jail the first time that Terry met her. He later told me that he thought Morag was "a rather mercurial girl, as cute as cute as she could be, with a tremendous wit about her. And she could out-talk most lawyers."

The court in Austin had arranged for some psychological tests to be carried out, which was standard practice in Texas. Terry told us later that during one of the sessions the psychologist asked Morag "When is Thanksgiving Day?" Morag had replied with a short "Why do you want to know that?" Rather perturbed, the psychologist said "It is one of the standard questions that you need to answer." As sharp as anything Morag had looked the person straight in the eye and asked "Fine, when is Boxing Day?" The rather confused psychologist could only manage a curt reply. "I don't know, but you are supposed to answer the Thanksgiving question." Morag, in her most dominant and determined tone, with a hint of Scottish directness, retorted "I don't have any idea when Thanksgiving is. We don't celebrate that where I live." Morag passed the psychological test!

Terry was right. Morag was sharp, and very clever. And she could certainly talk the rear-end off most people! But had she done enough? Had she managed to convince the jury that she should be given custody and that Jasmine should be allowed to return to Scotland? At that point, I just didn't know.

Terry Weeks had thought the case was a difficult one. Later he commented that he considered the case "not much of a winner". Thankfully I didn't know that at the time. He thought that Judge Dietz, the presiding judge, had been very angry with Morag because she tried to abduct Jasmine from the state of Texas and had fled to California. Because Morag would be seen by the judge as a "bad girl" Terry had called his strategy for defending her "a bad dog defence".

I never understood what Terry had meant by the "bad dog defence" until I read a book several years later, written by a Scottish journalist. Alastair Bisset covered the case in Austin on behalf of the Scottish regional *Press & Journal* newspaper, lovingly known as the *P&J*. Bisset wrote a paragraph in his book about the Terry Weeks style of defence. He had interviewed Terry, who told him the story of a "bad dog".

Terry told Bisset "I had a dog that used to raid the trash can when I was at work. When I got home I would spank the dog and put his nose in the trash and I would yell at him. Finally, the dog got the point. When I came home the dog would meet me at the front door, roll over and pee on himself. The dog knew that raiding the trash can was bad but he just couldn't stop himself. When you see your dog rolling over and peeing on himself, all you can do is say 'it's okay, chum, we can sort this out together'. Morag was the bad dog and we are going to tell the jury that. But we are also going to get Morag to convince the jury that she is truly sorry and that she can change."

Oh Morag, I so hoped that she could change and that the three of us would be going home soon to give her the chance for that change to happen.

I thought back to the closing arguments of Terry Weeks. Only a few hours ago I had listened to him tell the jury that "Jasmine needs protection". Terry kept eye contact with the members of the jury as he said "She needs protection from that woman over there. This little girl was healthy. She was doing all right in the UK, until she was ordered by some English court to get over here on the basis of a lying declaration, given by Mr Chapman. Ladies and gentlemen, the declaration that Jasmine had lived with Mr Chapman for six months, thereby warranting his claim over custody of his daughter, is false."

It had been a crazy situation. An English court had decided that Jasmine should be taken from Morag's arms to go to the US. The English judge ruled that, ultimately, it was the court in Austin that should decide whether or not her father, Marcus Chapman, should have custody of the little girl. A wee girl, born in Scotland, to a Scottish mother, and who lived in Scotland most of her life, had been ordered to go to America by an English judge to face a jury. That jury would decide whether the girl was to live in the US or the UK. Even today I can't help wondering if a Scottish judge would have made a different decision. Would a Scottish judge have been taken in by the lies of the Chapman family? As a born-and-bred Scot, I certainly would have hoped not.

"That woman", to whom Terry had referred, was Marcus' mother, Lawilda Chapman. She had helped Marcus build a case against Morag to get custody of the little girl. That was what this fight had been all about.

"Is she safe in England?" Terry rhetorically asked the jury. I think he meant "would she be safe in Scotland?", but the Americans have trouble with the whole English/Scottish thing. He went on to elaborate. "She will be. They have people that go out and look after you. They are pretty intensive about child care over there and they think that mothers ought to stay at home until the child is five or six. That's a social deal. This child was developmentally okay. Nobody had any problems with her because she was doing just fine. Her mother, Morag, was well trained as a nurse. She had certificates in child care, to do child placement work, and to train mothers how to raise kids. Jasmine was doing just fine, until we stepped in and tried to help. Our help has hurt this little girl."

Those were strong words from Terry. The jury had kept an intent eye on him the whole time he was addressing them. I watched each member of the jury and they all seemed to be hanging on his every word.

Terry Weeks had been right when he said that Morag had been trained well. She had gone to college in Scotland to study child care and she was a natural with kids. She was a good mother too. Yes, she had had her problems in her own personal life, but who doesn't. Jasmine and Morag were made for each other, and I never ever feared for Jasmine when Morag was around. There is a special bond between every mother and daughter, but the bond that Morag had with little Jasmine was extra-special. I could see it in the little girl's eyes every time her mummy was near. They loved each other so very much.

I was on holiday in Turkey when Morag called to tell me the news that I had just become a grandmother. At just over five pounds, little Jasmine entered the world on 25 May 1992 at Aberdeen Maternity Hospital, which happened to be the birthday of my Aunty Mary. I asked Morag why she had decided on the name Jasmine. Morag said that when she was a little girl of 11, she remembered smelling a wonderful scent. Her uncle had told her that the smell was the plant jasmine, which is a member of the olive family of shrubs. Morag said she loved that smell and she loved her daughter so Jasmine it would be.

Morag and Marcus christened their daughter Jasmine Jamee Chapman. Marcus had insisted that he wanted his daughter to have his father's name so they agreed that Jamee sounded better than Jimmy, which was the name that his dad, James Chapman, was known as.

When I arrived back from my holiday I made a beeline to see my granddaughter. Her little face topped with black hair was beautiful. I held her in my arms and thought of the joy of the many years to come. A happy family with a young gorgeous girl, I thought, what more could Morag and Marcus want. Little did I know that just over three years later I would be trying to comfort my daughter while waiting for a court in the US to decide the fate of her child.

Terry Weeks made an interesting comment during his summation. When he talked about Morag and Jasmine he talked about their love and their bond. But he also talked about Lawilda and Jimmy Chapman. He said "They are not bad people, are they? They are grandparents, they have a granddaughter. They have two sons of their own. Maybe they wanted a daughter of their own. You all watched Lawilda and you heard her testimony in this court. Remember, she said that she told Morag during her pregnancy that she would 'take that child away from you before it is even born'." But Terry Weeks was astute enough to realise that Jasmine and Lawilda didn't have a bond, not like Jasmine and Morag. Terry said "The bond isn't there very much. The child bonded with the grandfather, perhaps a warmer person, rather than with Lawilda."

Sitting in that apartment I couldn't help thinking about the possible outcome that might put little Jasmine into the hands of the Chapmans. If the court returned a verdict whereby the Chapmans got custody, little Jasmine would have to grow up with a family that seemed cold and unloving. Yes, they had money and they certainly knew how much money could talk. But Lawilda didn't realise that money cannot buy love. That was what she was attempting to do, but Terry saw through her. I just hoped the jury did too.

Why had Lawilda taken a dislike to Morag? I don't know. It was a real mystery to me. I never really liked Lawilda myself. Jimmy was a little different. He was charismatic and quite friendly. He had fought during the war and had risen to the rank of Lieutenant Colonel, had flown helicopters and been injured as well. He was a stereotypical American hero. The jury liked him, I could tell. They seemed to warm to his good-boy profile. He was a war veteran, a pillar of the community and, maybe, soon to be legal guardian of my little granddaughter.

The Chapmans had money. They could take care of Jasmine. They could give her anything she wanted. But they couldn't give her true love, not the sort of love that Morag could give her daughter. I stared out of that apartment window in Red River Street and prayed that the jury would see beyond money. But this was America. A country that is big on money and a country where money talks. And this was Texas, where money really talks!

The Chapman family had invested their money in property. Marcus, Morag and Jasmine had decided to move from Scotland to Austin nine months after Jasmine was born. Marcus had worked in the oil and gas industry but had decided that he wanted to manage the Chapman's property business. This meant that they had to move from the UK to the US. On the plus side was the fact that Marcus could be a full-time dad, rather than having to work offshore for long periods of time. Morag was convinced that their daughter needed a steady family environment so she made the sacrifice of a move to the US so that her daughter could be raised in a stable family.

Unfortunately, the relationship between Morag and Marcus quickly deteriorated. At one stage, Morag called a child-abuse line after she said that Marcus hit Jasmine with a telephone receiver. Morag told me that she had been subjected to violent attacks by Marcus.

Lawilda didn't help the situation. Morag told me that Lawilda kept interfering in their lives. Marcus was constantly asking his mother for advice and he seemed to take her side on everything. Morag had told him "Stand up for yourself. If there are things that need to be discussed that involve Jasmine then it's me you should come to, not your mother."

Realising their relationship was beyond repair, Morag planned to take little Jasmine from their home in Austin back to the UK. Morag was doing nothing illegal. Jasmine was Scottish and not American. Marcus could not claim that he had custodial rights because, according to Texas law, a person must have spent six months in the state before they could be classed as s citizen. Morag had every right to leave the US with her little daughter.

However, Morag's plan didn't go quite the way she thought it might have. Marcus got wind of Morag's intention to leave the US. He took his daughter, who was now just over 12 months old, and vanished. Thinking that Marcus would have taken the girl to Lawilda, Morag made the 200-mile trip to the Chapman's house, but alas there was no sign of the child.

Panic-stricken, Morag had contacted the British Consulate-General in Houston and explained the situation. Of course, they had no jurisdiction because no offence had really been committed. However, a kindly lady gave Morag some important advice. Convinced that the father would return his daughter, the lady at the Consulate-General told Morag to barricade herself in her home until someone bought a flight ticket out of the country. She told Morag to buy enough food for a few days and to stay in the house.

Morag took the lady's advice. She wrote a cheque for $200 at a local supermarket, unaware that Marcus had cleared her bank account of all money. On the same day Marcus eventually showed up with Jasmine. Without explanation where he had taken the little girl, he simply handed Jasmine back to her mother. Morag sat it out for a few days until flight tickets were organised. She and Jasmine left for the UK.

Of course, when the supermarket presented their cheque to the bank it bounced and an official complaint was made to the police. Officers started to look into the matter and issued an arrest warrant for Morag. But it was too late. Morag and Jasmine had returned to the UK.

But Marcus never gave up. After several years of legal correspondence across the Atlantic Ocean, an English court ordered Jasmine to go to Texas.

The final words of Terry Weeks during his summation in the court that afternoon kept ringing in my ears. Over and over again, as I busied myself in that little apartment, I could hear him as his gaze penetrated into the souls of each of the jury members. "What can be done at this point because we have an awful separation of this little girl's family? The child needs to be given the opportunity to have two citizenships so that she can enjoy summers in the United States and summers in Scotland. She needs to have an extended family on both sides. She needs that so that she can be a whole person. If you cut off one family you may as well cut her leg off. The Chapmans have money so they can travel back and forth to Scotland. But if Morag is sent back to Scotland without her daughter with these criminal charges behind her there will be no way for her to get back to see her daughter. Yes, if the Chapmans get custody Jasmine will have a grandmother and various aunts and maybe a stepmother one day. But she won't have a mother."

Terry Weeks said "She has been well raised in Scotland. She was a normal happy little kid until we started 'helping out'. We are asking you to help out again. We are asking you to award custody of Jasmine to Morag Dodds."

Terry's words were poignant. They were strong. They were true. But would they make any difference? The Chapmans had spent a huge amount of money on this case. I could only hope that the jury were not swayed by wealth. But this was America!

I found out later that the *P&J* in Aberdeen had run a feature on the final day of the trial. Ironic to think that, while Morag and I were sitting waiting in the apartment, people at home would have read about the closing day of the trial. Alastair Bisset, the journalist covering the case, clearly thought that the Chapman family were moving the emphasis on who should look after Jasmine. The report read:

<display begins>

Texas child-care authorities want Aberdeen-born tug-of-love toddler Jasmine Dodds to remain in America. They claim this is the only way the two year old will be guaranteed a stable and secure future. But Jasmine's grandmother, Forres horse-breeder Flora Dempster, told the child-custody trial in the Texas state capital of Austin, 'If Jasmine is allowed back home to Scotland, she will get all the support she needs.'

The claim that Jasmine would be better off in Texas was made by the court-appointed child welfare officer who has been monitoring the case since last September. She told the jury that neither of Jasmine's parents were fit to look after the youngster.

'They are both very immature and lack judgement,' she said. 'I don't think they have the stability to put Jasmine's needs before their own.'

The court-appointed child welfare officer said that, in her opinion, Jasmine's future should be with Marcus' parents who live in the small town of Woodville, 200 miles south of Austin. Both are full-time teachers.

Marcus' parents assured the jury they would provide the youngster with a secure home and that there would be no financial problems. Mr Chapman said that his wife would be willing to travel to Scotland on occasions so Jasmine could be reunited for short spells with her mother.

The child welfare officer told the court that Morag was obviously a loving and caring mother, but in her opinion had shown signs of having a serious drinking problem. Marcus, she said, had a very impulsive nature, a quick temper and was easily upset and angered.

During those few hours at the apartment, waiting for the phone to ring, I had felt myself day-dreaming. I had been thinking about Morag, Jasmine, Pip (Jasmine's pony) and my home in Scotland. How long would we have to wait in this place before we could find out what the future held for us all?

When they read the feature in the newspaper, people at home would clearly see that the Chapmans were after little Jasmine. I too could sense that Lawilda had upped her game. She was desperate to take the little girl. I could sense that we were losing.

And then the phone in that tiny apartment in Austin, Texas, rang.

A BIZZARE CASE AND LIP GLOSS

The verdict was in.

I ordered a taxi and we made the short journey to the court. Although it didn't take long to get from the apartment to the courthouse it was long enough for the brain to churn through the events of the last six days. How bizarre it all was. Six days ago, we sat in court on the first day of the trial as the attorneys interviewed each witness. Stuff like this could only happen in America!

I remember Alastair Bisset, the journalist from Scotland, telling me how ridiculous he thought the whole first day had been.

I first met Alastair after I made a frantic call to the *P&J* in Aberdeen a few months before the trial. I made the call just before Christmas. Morag had been arrested in the US and was in jail. She called me. I remember her last words to me on the phone, which were "help me, Mum."

What else could I do? I was thousands of miles away from her; she was in San Diego and I was in Forres in Scotland. The local paper in Aberdeen was my only hope. At least I was doing something. So I phoned the office of the *P&J* and pleaded with them to help us. They sent a journalist out to see me, on Christmas Eve. It was Alastair Bisset.

Alastair told me that this story had the potential to "run and run". He asked loads of questions and asked for photographs of Morag and Jasmine. I made a verbal deal with him that I would talk to no other newspaper and would consult only him before taking further action. He was really excited about this story. He knew that he had a scoop on his hands, maybe even Journalist of the Year! Regarding the money, I knew the *P&J* didn't pay for these types of stories, which didn't bother me in the slightest. All I wanted was for people to know what was going on and for my fellow Scots to get behind us and to give Morag support.

Alastair made a "secret" call to Morag. He managed to get through to the women's prison in San Diego where they were holding her before transporting her back to Texas. Morag had fled to Stuart, her brother and my only son, who was living in San Diego at the time. Alastair said to Morag "Hello, this is Uncle Alastair, from the *P&J* shop in Aberdeen." Nobody in San Diego would have understood the "code" but Morag had picked up on it at once. She was smart. She knew that Alastair was talking to her in a coded sort of way. Alastair managed to get the information he needed to run his first story.

On a daily basis, the *P&J* continued to run features about the "North-east Tug-of Love" that was taking place on the other side of the Atlantic.

Alastair was right. That first day in court was unusual to say the least. Each potential juror was grilled by the various lawyers. They were asked really personal questions about their sexual orientation, their work, religious and political beliefs.

Bizarre ways in Texas!

It was quite funny in a strange sort of way. Terry Weeks asked them "You all know about Bluebell Creamery?" When they all nodded their heads and uttered "yea", or "sure man" he went on to ask "Do you know how many distilleries are in Scotland?"

Each of the jurors kept looking at me when he started rambling on about Scots people drinking and about Hadrian's Wall. He said "Scotland is smaller than Texas and we have one distillery. They have 270! They drink all they can and sell the rest. Have you heard about Hadrian's

Wall? They had to build that because the English couldn't handle the Scots people. The Scots used to crawl over the wall and behave like bad people. They don't always follow the rules."

I couldn't believe what he was saying but actually he was preparing the jury for what was about to come. By the time that Terry had started to talk about Morag and her drinking, the jurors were firmly of the belief that all Scots drink heavily and run around like savages!

What Terry did during that first morning was strange but he was trying to get the "junk" out before he started telling them that Morag was a good mother. Sure, she had been arrested and sure, she did have a drink habit, but Terry wanted to build up the fact that Morag was a loving mother. The "bad dog defence" had started.

One of the jurors was dismissed because he was one of the policemen who had arrested Morag when her cheque bounced. Another juror told Terry "I went for custody of my daughter when my marriage broke up, but my daughter missed her mother so much that I had to return the child to her." He was a major plus for Morag's case but unfortunately the Chapman's attorney's managed to get him stood down.

Judge Dietz was a character too. Morag had a security tag on her ankle when she walked into the court. The judge said "I don't want people in this court with a uniform on. To my mind, that tag is a uniform. Are there any objections?"

Of course, the Chapman army of attorneys all protested, advising the judge that Morag might flee the court if she wasn't tagged. Judge Dietz replied "Who says she's going to boogie? Why are you objecting? You think she's going to boogie? She boogies, she loses the child. Is that right? She boogies, she will lose her case. Now, get that off." A stunned court raised no further objections.

The judge asked one of the jurors if he had any stickers on his car. The perplexed man could only shake his head.

The judge simply wanted to know if the man had any strong feelings about anything. Bizarre!

The *P&J* ran a story about the opening day of the trial. It read

<display begins>

'It is like having a prisoner in prison clothes in my court. I don't want that,' said Judge John Dietz, who will be presiding at the week-long custody case in Austin, Texas, which will determine the future of Morag's two-year-old daughter Jasmine. 'She does not have the child with her, and there is no way she is going to abscond,' he said. 'She has every incentive in the world to stay right here in Texas.'

Last night a delighted Morag said, 'I will be glad to see the back of that bracelet. It is the one piece of jewellery I can do without.' Earlier, Judge Dietz warned lawyers involved in the case, 'There had better not be any goddam hot potatoes in this courtroom this week. If there is, I am going to hurt you all a little bit.'

His decision to allow Morag (31) to shed the electronic ankle bracelet she had had to wear since being freed on bail last month came after a request from her lawyer Terry Weeks. The device had restricted her to the confines of her tiny apartment, where she was monitored regularly by the court authorities after being brought back from California following her abduction of Jasmine.

A 12-strong jury will be asked to decide later this week whether Aberdeen-born Jasmine returns home to Scotland with her mother or remains in Texas with her father Marcus Chapman (35), Morag's former boyfriend.

In a no-holds-barred three-hour session with the five lawyers involved in the case Judge Dietz discarded his official robes, picked up a red felt-tip pen and walked to a display board in the court to map out proceedings. He made it clear that he wanted the case to be resolved by the end of the week. 'I am going to scare you, and you are all going to start screaming, but I am going to limit you all to four hours' questioning each,' he said.

In exchanges that would not happen in a Scottish court, the judge told the lawyers, 'I hope you will all be able to be sweet with one another.'

The jury will be selected this morning and evidence in the case will get underway later in the day. Texas is the only state in America where juries are involved in child-custody cases.

<display ends>

The opening day was stressful for all of us. I think Morag held up quite well under the pressure of the start of the trial. Regarding the other days the pace seemed to ebb and flow. The attorneys took a lot of time discussing technical and legal issues and they laboured the point with many witnesses.

Another bizarre thing that happened was the bounced cheque. They had this huge blackboard in the courtroom and they produced a copy of the cheque, blown up to about four times its normal size.

Encouragingly, after Morag gave evidence, Terry said "She did brilliantly." Anything that the other side could throw at her she was able to put right back. But, she was asked up a second time and that didn't go too well. I wasn't sure, but I suspected that Morag and Randy, my attorney, might have been having a fling. During the second time that Morag had to give evidence she was not quite as confident as she had been the first time. Afterwards she told me that it was because Randy's wife had come into the courtroom. Morag thought that maybe Randy's wife had suspected something going on between them and that was why she decided to visit the court. After Morag gave evidence Terry had said "God, I don't know what went wrong with her. We had her winning the case after she was on the first time, but this next time was such a mess."

I had asked Randy Berry to represent me in the case, more to keep a watching brief on what was going on during the whole legal process. Another reason for having a lawyer of my own was because in the US courts can award custody to grandparents so I thought it might be a good idea to have my own representative. So we had Terry, who was doing the whole courtroom thing, and Randy, who was representing me.

Randy visited us a few times at our apartment while we were waiting for the trial date to be set. I didn't suspect that Morag and Randy were doing anything other than exchanging legal talk, but maybe they had been.

Randy was quite good looking, and he did take an instant liking to Morag, who was beautiful, slim and blonde. Randy actually looked a bit like John Cleese.

My testimony in court went quite well. I thought I was going to be in for a really hard time and put under a lot of pressure. But they didn't challenge me too much. They asked me about bringing up my kids, Morag and Stuart, and about family life when they were growing up. One point I did make was to emphasise that I had always wanted my kids to have confidence. I think it is important for a mother to instil confidence in her children because it is a big, bad and nasty world out there. Let them go so they can get on with their lives was my approach. Always be there for them but teach them how to survive. Morag certainly was a survivor.

When the Chapman's attorneys asked me what I had given my children when they were growing up, I had replied emphatically "confidence to let go and not to be tied to their mother's apron strings, and to go and see how other people live their lives." It had been unfortunate for Marcus that Jimmy Ross and Lawilda hadn't done the same with him because he was still very much tied to his parents.

One positive thing that happened during the trial was Don Evans. Don had flown over from Scotland to support us. He was my partner at the time so he wanted to do something to help out. He was really fond of Jasmine and she took well to Don too.

Don had been involved in social work in the UK for many years and Terry Weeks thought that he would make a good "expert" witness. The Chapman's lawyers had been told that a witness would be produced but Terry had managed to keep it relatively low key. In the US, both sides usually take depositions, which must be made available to the other side. Depositions, which are legal documents that can be referred to in court, are done before the trial starts. However, Terry's game plan with Don was to spring a surprise on the other side so that they didn't have time to take a deposition. I don't know how it all works in the US but Terry clearly had a plan – and it worked quite well.

I keep using the word "bizarre" but this was another example of it. Terry Weeks wanted to keep Don hidden away. Don wanted to hire a car but Terry thought this was a risk. He thought that, if the other side had a private detective snooping around outside the Red River Street apartment, they might spot Don coming out of a hire car and report back to the Chapmans. So a convoluted arrangement was made for Don to get use of a car. Someone else hired it and Don was given a loan of the car. Seems strange, but that's the US.

Don, who qualified as a doctor before changing careers to social work, swotted up on all sorts of research about child psychology and child care. He went to the Perry-Castaneda library in Austin and spent a week reading. All his hard work paid off tremendously. Terry said later that Don had spoken with authority and with confidence in the courtroom. Clearly, the Chapman camp was shaken by Don's expert testimony. Don spoke about why Jasmine should be allowed to settle with her mother and he passionately stated how devastating it would be for

Jasmine's future if she were to be forced to stay in the US with the Chapman family.

Terry Weeks grinned when he told me his plan for Don. He had said "When I asked the judge if it was okay to put old Don on the stand, he, and the Chapman lawyers thought he was going to appear as a character witness only, saying something like 'yea, I'm Don, Flora's boyfriend, and I think Flora and Morag are great.' Little did the Chapman camp know Don was to drive a wedge through their case.

Terry later said "The jury sat mesmerised during Don's presentation. He talked about some research paper that he had found, something from the World Health Organisation first written in 1948. Don went on and on about the modern approach to child care and about his work in the Social Department in Scotland. He was brilliant. It was brutal!"

Don couldn't hang around to wait for the verdict because he had to get back to Scotland to sort out some of his own personal stuff. He left immediately after he gave his testimony.

If we thought that Don had managed to score some points for us at the trial, then the mysterious "letters" arriving could have taken out all the good work he did. Because the *P&J* newspaper was reporting events in Austin on a daily basis, the trial would have intrigued many people in Forres. Not all of those people would have been happy to read about the events taking place across the Atlantic. Somehow, an old newspaper clipping had made it across the Atlantic and into the courtroom in Austin.

Many years before the case, I had allowed some homeless friends to park their caravans on my land. Unfortunately, one of those people was fined for growing cannabis plants. The local newspaper had reported the story, giving my address as the abode of the person fined £100. The headline in the newspaper boldly stated "Caught with Cannabis in Caravan." Someone had copied the old newspaper clipping and had sent it to the court in Austin, with some additional words scribbled alongside it "One of Dempster's tenants. Could only find this one. There have been others. Some of Dempster's tenants live in caravans on her ground, others live in her actual home where Jasmine is."

The same anonymous writer had gone to considerable trouble to collect and copy other newspaper items concerning court appearances in which the accused had given their addresses as a caravan site on land occupied by Don Evan's antiques business.

In another letter, which was unsigned, vicious allegations about the private lives of Don and me were made. Those letters, postmarked "Elgin", a town a few miles from Forres, were also sent to the Mayor of Austin, and to Lawilda Chapman. Thankfully, those letters were not admissible in court because the content of them and the allegations made could not be corroborated. However, some soul at home obviously had taken a dislike to me and had tried to derail the court case.

Those letters amused and beguiled Terry Weeks. He told me later "This case was truly bizarre. There were twists and turns at every corner." He went on to tell me another funny story, one that he was quite intrigued by. He said that he was worried about the Chapman's lawyers continually banging on about Morag's drinking problems and that she couldn't give up alcohol. Terry had made a point of staying with her all day so that he could keep an eye on her.

One day, Terry had smelled alcohol on Morag and accused her of drinking. Morag vociferously denied it. Terry asked her, "Well, what's that I can smell on you?" Morag told him about the lip gloss that she uses, stuff that can't be bought in the US. It has a strong smell, similar to alcohol.

Morag was called back to the stand to answer some more questions by the Chapman's lawyers. Terry approached Morag on the stand to cross-examine and he said to her "I asked you earlier if you had been drinking and you said no. I then asked you why you smelled as though you had alcohol on your breath and you said it might have been lip gloss. Is this it?" Terry produced a small container of lip gloss, marked 'Respondent's Exhibit 15'.

Well, Judge Dietz was furious. He said "Stop. Come up here. Weeks, you are not getting that exhibit into evidence." A heated exchange took place between the judge and Terry Weeks. They were arguing about whether this lip gloss could be admissible evidence. Eventually, Terry said to Morag "Why don't you put some of that lip gloss on your lips and walk by the jury?" Bemused, Judge Dietz told her "Leave the witness box, apply the lip seal and get as close as you can to kissing the members of the jury."

As Morag walked back and forth in front of the jury, Terry Weeks sprang to his feet and said "I offer exhibit 15". The lip gloss now had to be admitted because it had been displayed to the jury in a demonstration. The judge was very mad at Weeks.

I couldn't help but think how crazy the court system is in the US. Would this have happened in a Scottish court?

Bizarre!

A SCOTTISH GIRL IN ENGLAND AND
A DOG CALLED FROSTIE

At long last, our time in that apartment in Red River Street was coming to an end. All I could think about was getting back to the courtroom and finding out what the verdict was going to be. Hopefully, Morag, Jasmine and I would be leaving for Scotland and we could say goodbye to this nightmare, and to this cramped apartment, which we had occupied together since I arrived in Austin, goodness knows how many weeks ago. It seemed like a lifetime since I had stepped off the plane, on a mission to help support my daughter through, I thought, what would be the worst time of her life.

Morag was an enterprising type of person, always had been, so I knew that she would fight for her little girl in every way possible. And I was going to fight with her.

I flew out to Austin in January 1995. I travelled through Schiphol Airport in Amsterdam and I remember a security official asking me if this was a business or leisure trip. I replied "I don't know, I am going to try to get my daughter out of jail."

Randy Berry had contacted me the month before to let me know that Morag had ended up in prison in San Diego and that the Chapmans had temporary custody of Jasmine.

On 26 December 1994, the *P&J* ran a lengthy feature on the front page of the newspaper. Under the headline "Snatch Mum in US Prison Nightmare" the feature quoted me as saying

This past week has been a nightmare. How can anyone keep a mother from being with her baby daughter, especially at Christmas time? Morag must be heartbroken, and I can't even get to speak to her on the telephone. It does not bear thinking about. I only wish I had gone out to America earlier to give her moral support. She has been driven too far, and I am obviously concerned for her mental state. Now it appears that the only way my daughter will see her child again is if I raise an action for custody. Under Texas law, I have the right to do this.

<display ends>

Marcus Chapman and his family were determined not to be left out of the limelight. The *P&J* carried a quote from him two days later, which read

<display begins>

Jasmine is doing real fine just now. She is looking good and is perfectly happy. Morag and I have split up. She has not proved to be a good mother. She has had her problems for a long time. The custody fight over Jasmine has been going on for a long time, and I just hope we are now coming to an end.

<display ends>

This statement to the press was from a man who, I believe, ordered his first wife to have an abortion because their marriage was breaking down, and he threatened to kill her if she didn't go through with the termination.

So, that's why I found myself out in Texas, to help Morag win back little Jasmine. I knew it was going to be tough, especially since Morag was currently in prison in San Diego. How had that happened? Perhaps if I had flown out much earlier she might not have gone on the run. The stress of the whole thing had been too much for her and she clearly hadn't been thinking straight.

When I stepped off that plane in Texas I knew we had a really tough fight on our hands, especially since we were going to be up against the Chapmans, who not only had money to buy attorneys but also had a strong desire to rob Morag of her daughter. Right from the start of this whole case the Chapmans had made no secret of their intentions, and they had started their fight as soon as Morag had returned to the UK after her split-up with Marcus.

Morag had been really happy after returning to Britain. She decided to stay with her father rather than with me in Forres. Her father had property that wasn't being used in Northumberland so it was convenient for Morag to stay there.

Two months after returning from Texas, Morag was allocated a two-bedroom council house in the new town of Killingworth, near Newcastle upon Tyne. Life was certainly picking up for her, and she seemed to be enjoying the freedom from Texas, Marcus and Lawilda Chapman. Instead of the screams and violence that Jasmine had been exposed to in Austin, their new home was full of laughter, joy and happiness.

However, danger continued to lurk. Morag had become almost paranoid about Marcus snatching Jasmine. She had told me "They will be back. Mark my words, Mum, they will be back, and I am scared for Jasmine." Such was her paranoia that Morag wanted Jasmine to learn to swim, so that if she ever ended up back in Marcus' house near the lake in Austin, she would be able to swim if she got into difficulty in the lake.

Jack Reeves worked offshore, on oil rigs and on supply vessels that carried cargo and supplies to the oil and gas fields in the North Sea. Morag had met Jack when she worked on the rigs herself. Jack would often visit Morag and Jasmine at their home in Killingworth, becoming almost a father-figure to the little girl.

Uncle Jack was the bee's knees according to Jasmine. She adored him. He was kind to Morag too, because he knew that money was tight and that she needed help with supporting the little girl. He knew too, that Jasmine's father was conspicuous by his absence. At Christmas, in 1993, no presents, nor even a card, arrived from Texas. This disgusted Jack.

I personally was never a fan of Jack. But we did have two things in common. Firstly, Jack seemed to care for Morag and he certainly adored Jasmine. The second thing that we agreed on was our disgust for the Chapmans and for Marcus in particular. However, I never really trusted him because I always thought he had a "hidden agenda". My view was that Jack thought if he could get close to Jasmine, Morag would come with the deal.

I couldn't believe that Marcus would ignore his daughter at Christmas-time. Not even a card, even although Morag had continued to send photographs of Jasmine to show how she was growing and developing.

I didn't trust Lawilda and Jimmy Ross either. My suspicions were further solidified when I found out they wanted to visit England to see their granddaughter.

Morag allowed them to stay at her place in Killingworth. She even gave up her bedroom so the Chapmans could stay with her. The site of her little house, packed into a street with other similar houses, must have been quite a shock to the Chapmans. They were used to sprawling Texas farmland, with acres of free space around their homes. Seeing their granddaughter growing up in what they probably considered a "shanty town" was too much for them to bear.

The Chapmans stayed with Morag and Jasmine for a few days. They took Jasmine to a park but the little girl wasn't allowed to mix and play with the other children in the park. Council kids weren't good enough for Lawilda so she stopped Jasmine from playing with them.

I was convinced their trip to England was a spying mission rather than a holiday to see their granddaughter. Morag was happy. Jasmine was happy. But I was convinced that things were going to take a turn for the worse following Lawilda and Jimmy Ross returning to the States. I couldn't have been more right.

Morag asked a lawyer to write a letter to Neal Pfeiffer, Marcus' legal representative in Texas. The letter basically set out Morag's intention to seek a residence order, which is a simple way of laying down the premise that the child will live with her mother. The letter advised Marcus that Morag had no intention of permitting him from keeping in contact with his daughter and visiting her whenever he wanted to, providing arrangements for travel were made in advance.

On 10 January 1994, Morag received a letter from Neal Pfeiffer, a letter that she had dreaded might arrive one day. It made it very clear that Marcus was heading for a fight. A series of exchanges were made by both legal representatives, and each letter seemed to raise the heat.

A very distraught Morag called me and said "Marcus says it would be better for Jasmine to live with him. They are going to ask the courts in England to rule that Jasmine be allowed to spend her summer holidays in Austin, with the Chapmans and that she should have every second Christmas in Texas too. Why was he doing this, Mum? He has ignored us both for so long, now he wants Jasmine. I don't trust him. If he takes Jasmine for a holiday to the US I will never see her again."

As the winter rolled on, and the snow started to fall in Tyneside in England, another storm was brewing. Morag, in tears, called me. She said "I have had another letter. Marcus has hired a lawyer in London and they are demanding my address. Morag had been summoned to attend a hearing in London.

With tears in her eyes, Morag told her little girl "I have to go away for a few days to tell some important people that I love you. If I manage to do that, I will buy you a nice present, a dog. Would you like that?" To gasps of joy from the little girl, Morag left for London.

Thankfully, the High Court judge ruled in favour of Morag, with the stipulation that Marcus be given "reasonable" access to the child. She headed home to her daughter as happy as could be. And, an addition to their family was made, Frostie, the most beautiful mixed-breed dog that Morag had ever seen.

The battle had been won, but the war was far from over.

Marcus appealed the judge's decision. Not only did he want a review of the High Court decision but he wanted to throw a real curve-ball into the mix. Marcus declared that the case should be heard by a Texas judge, not an English one.

Morag couldn't believe all of this, and neither could I. Jasmine was Scottish, she was living with her mother in England and an English court had made a decision. How could anyone possibly agree with Marcus and the Chapmans that a court thousands of miles away should be asked to decide on custody? He argued that Jasmine was an American citizen because she had lived in America for more than six months. That was the basis of his argument. I was confident that no court in Europe would agree to this. How wrong was I?

If only Morag had taken my advice and moved back to Scotland. I was sure that this was the reason she was having such an unsympathetic time from the English courts. Morag told me later that, had she been advised by her lawyers that it would be better living in Scotland, she would have made the move immediately. But, although her family and friends, including me, had pleaded with her to move north of the border, she had remained in Tyneside, in England. A Scottish court, in my opinion, would never have entertained a Scottish mother, with a Scottish child, living in Scotland, having to go through a possible separation from her daughter. However, Morag stayed in England and therefore the English courts had jurisdiction. Until, that is, Marcus got his way.

The dreaded summons arrived.

As the summer months neared, Morag was informed that an appeal hearing would be held in London.

Of all the crazy and stupid things that have happened in my life, I think the decision made by those appeal judges has to be one of the most ridiculous, unsympathetic and downright wrong. Morag lost the appeal and was ordered to let Jasmine go to the US so that a Texas court could decide who was to get custody. A very Scottish girl being told by an English court that she now faced a decision in Texas, it just beggared belief.

Only one thing was in Morag's favour. Her lawyers managed to get the judge to order Marcus to care for Morag and Jasmine when they were awaiting trial in Texas. Marcus had to pay for the flights, find accommodation in a "reasonable" area of Austin for Morag and Jasmine and pay $1200 every month as maintenance while they were in the US. He had to provide a car as well and, more importantly, the judge said that the child should not be removed from her mother during their time in the state.

Knowing that the case in America could drag on for months, Morag decided to inform the housing authority that she was leaving and that they could have their house back. The person she spoke to was sympathetic and told her she would be placed on the priority list again when she returned. Emphatically, Morag said "Oh, I'll be back, but not to England. I have made that mistake once, and it will never happen again. I want to be among my own."

I hitched a horse trailer onto my car and headed from my home in Forres to Killingworth. When I reached Morag's house, I could see she had been crying and in a terrible state. Jack had travelled from his home in Fraserburgh to help pack up the house. Most of the furniture and goods would have to be sold to help pay for the legal fees that were inevitably going to accrue in the US. We quickly got to work emptying the house.

The next day, Jasmine, bewildered by what was going on, carried Frostie to my car. Jasmine had asked me to promise to look after her dog. A promise I made and a promise I so hoped that I could keep for the poor little girl. A girl, who should have been happy at home with mum, instead was being torn from her little world through no fault of her own. At the hands of adults who should have known better, little Jasmine was heading for the unknown. Court judges, appeal judges and even her real family had failed her.

As I drove back to Scotland, knowing that Morag and Jasmine were on their way across the Atlantic, I thought about all the "if only's". If only Morag had moved to Scotland. If only she hadn't started the ball rolling with that first letter to Marcus. If only Lawilda and Jimmy Ross had put Jasmine first instead of their own selfishness. Far too many "if only's".

I am a strong person. I have always been a strong person. I think my strength comes from the Macdonald genes that I inherited. I have always been able to put on a brave face and meet a crisis head on. But not then. Somewhere on the road from Newcastle upon Tyne to the Scottish Borders, as a jet with my two girls on board flew across the sky, I lost my strength. I pulled over, stopped the car and broke down crying.

Frostie woke up. My thoughts turned to him. I cleared my eyes, started the car and somewhere on that summer's night, I found my strength again. I knew I needed to be strong, for this was just the start of a long and arduous road. Not the road home, but the road that would take us on a challenging journey in the US, a fight against selfishness and a fight against all those money-bought attorneys paid for by the Chapmans.

I got home to Forres, unpacked the trailer and headed back down to Killingworth for a second load. Jack was with me this time and that was an ordeal in itself, for he talked constantly about Jack. Jack and more Jack.

Morag had arrived in Austin. Randy, my legal representative, told me later what one of the judges had said when proceedings in the US had got underway, now that Morag and Jasmine had arrived. The judge said "Miss Dodds, I really don't know why you are here. We do not have jurisdiction in custody matters over a citizen of the United Kingdom. But if they don't want it, then we'll have to take it. If your country won't take responsibility, then I guess we'll have to."

I think he got that right. An English court pandered to the demands of a Texan with money. And, the audacity of it too was that the court awarded the cowboy from Texas Legal Aid! A court that should have taken responsibility failed to do so. I urged Morag to turn about and come home, and to let a Scottish court take on the battle. But her attitude was, well, I'm here now, so I had better'd just get on with it. I was upset with my daughter, but at the same time I was very, very proud of her. Mothers fight for their children, but Morag seemed to be going the extra mile. She had made sacrifice upon sacrifice to protect Jasmine, and now she was making even more sacrifices. She was strong, or so I thought, and she was a fighter. I was very proud of my girl. I think she inherited the Macdonald genes as well.

Jack Reeves had made a trip out to see Morag and Jasmine. He had come off the rigs and flown out to Austin. Jack and Morag talked into the wee small hours. But that night, the apartment where Morag was staying was stormed by police. Apparently, the police had received a tip-off about Morag being in the US; she was still wanted for the "bounced cheque" episode from the last time she was in Texas.

It was warm in the apartment. Jack had on his jeans but no shirt, and Jasmine, because she was suffering from the heat and humidity, was lying naked on top of her bed. When the police came into the room, all they saw was a topless male standing beside a naked little girl. They assumed the worst and pounced upon him. Of course, it didn't help that Jack kept shouting "I will kill you" to the cops. Even now, events in that room are hazy. Jack is still in no doubt that he was beaten until he passed out. He was probably too drunk to remember.

Jack was arrested and spent the night in jail. He was fined $110 and allowed to go. He stayed in Austin for another two weeks before returning to Scotland.

However, the episode gave the Chapman camp ammunition. Morag was arrested too and questioned about the circumstances. Having a semi-naked man in the apartment where Marcus' daughter slept was grist to the mill of the Chapman lawyers. The events of that evening would be used against her time and time again.

As the weeks rolled by, the legal process in the US kept churning on and on. From our telephone calls, I could tell that Morag was falling deeper and deeper into despair. She had to tell her little Jasmine why they were there, why Jasmine couldn't play with the other kids and she had to tell her all of this not knowing when it would all end.

I spoke to Jasmine a few times. She always asked about her dog. With tears welling up in my eyes, I only hoped that I convinced her that Frostie was doing fine and that she would see him again very soon.

A PACK OF WOLVES AND BREAKING POINT

Morag called me quite regularly from Austin. I remember one of her first calls, when she said that she was bored already. But at least she had made some friends for Jasmine. Jake Harris, a neighbour at the apartment that Morag stayed in when she first arrived in Texas, became good friends with Morag. Although Jake was a divorcee, he often looked after his two children. Jasmine quickly made friends with Olivia and Helen, playing with them at the local park. Jake often took Morag back and forth to court because Marcus had failed to provide her with a car while in the US. Unlike Jack, Jake Harris had no hidden agenda with Morag; he simply wanted to help.

But things were soon to take yet another turn for the worse. A legal guardian is a person who has the legal authority to advise the courts about the personal interests of another person. Usually they are appointed where a minor or child is involved. A court will often appoint a legal guardian for an individual in need of special protection. In the United States of America, the term for a legal guardian is guardian *ad litem*, or GAL.

GALs in the US are often appointed to represent a child or minor in court proceedings. They have a lot of authority and they can make some very specific decisions regarding the child's care.

The one thing that I found surprising about the GAL process in the US was that qualifications of GALs vary quite a lot across the different states of America. Often, the appointed person does not need to have any experience nor do they require specific qualifications. They can sometimes be volunteers.

Randy had tried to get me appointed as Jasmine's Guardian, mainly to counteract attempts made by Lawilda and Jimmy Ross to be appointed as her guardians. However, the Juvenile Court of Travis County had decided that an independent person would be nominated as the GAL. Kathy Thomson, Jasmine's appointed GAL, was about 30 years of age, dressed like a man, and had, I think, a female partner. The walls in her office were adorned with pictures of her and another female arm-in-arm so I assumed she was gay. I don't have anything against gay people but I did think she was a strange choice as the Guardian *ad litem* of a child in the centre of a custody battle.

Morag often told me how she thought the Guardian *ad litem* had favoured the Chapmans. She also told me that the first time she and Marcus met Kathy, in her office, Marcus had offered to "buy" Morag out. He suggested giving her $22,000 for her to return to the UK and leave Jasmine behind. Of course, Morag refused. I am not sure what the GAL had said to this, but I got the impression from Morag that, had she agreed to take his money, Kathy Thomson would have gone along with it.

Morag's arrest was just what the Chapman camp needed and they were quick to take advantage of it. Within a few hours of Morag returning to her apartment, after being questioned by the police, Kathy Thomson intervened. Normally, in cases of violence or domestic dispute, the GAL would arrange for the affected child to be taken away from the parents and custody, on a temporary basis, given to relatives or friends. Morag had only one friend she could trust, Roberta Reid, whom she knew from her previous time in Austin. Morag gave Roberta's contact details to Kathy

Thomson, who arranged for Jasmine, once again, to be taken from her mother's arms.

In the US, the GAL has responsibility for determining whether the parent, or parents, is/are capable of looking after a child, and, more importantly, whether the child is at risk if they remained with the parent. After the Jack Reeves debacle, Kathy Thomson had talked to the police, neighbours, and Morag's attorney, Richard Jones, and she could not find any valid reason for Jasmine not to return to her mother.

So, at least for the time being, Jasmine was back with her mum. The wait for the trial continued.

Morag began the arduous task of giving statements to the attorneys, referred to as depositions in the US. Depositions are formally defined as "out-of-court oral testimony of a witness that is reduced to writing for later use in court". In all civil cases in the US depositions are conducted under Rule 30 of the *Federal Rules of Civil Procedure*, and most of the states, including Texas, use this system of information gathering. It sounds like a pretty straightforward part of the legal process. Depositions are usually taken in one of the attorney's offices. Like most people, I have watched television programmes that show the deposition process. On TV, the procedure looks amicable and fair.

Oh how wrong television can be!

William Powers, the attorney hired by Lawilda and Jimmy Ross Chapman, was considered to be one of the top legal professionals in the state. During the deposition process every reply given by Morag was critically analysed by Powers. He had one objective in mind, and that was to build up a case to prove Morag was an unfit mother. But Morag had done nothing wrong and she knew it. For the good of Jasmine, Morag endured hours of interrogation about her every move in the US. She was strong though.

She stuck it out, later being told that she had done an incredible job of handling all those tortuous questions.

Even Morag's friendship with Roberta had turned into a "window of opportunity" for that smart and evil attorney, Powers. Roberta's boyfriend, Warren, had paid a little too much attention to Morag. He started calling her late at night, asking her out on a date. Morag would have nothing to do with him, but Warren was persistent. Eventually, Morag had had enough and talked to Roberta about the advances being made by her boyfriend. Thinking that it would help to clear the air, Morag assumed that Roberta would be sympathetic and maybe confront Warren. Instead, she lashed out at Morag, breaking her two front teeth. Roberta also attacked Warren, and she even took an axe to his car windows.

Powers asked Morag why she hadn't filed charges against Roberta. Morag had actually filed charges but dropped them again after Roberta called her and suggested the two of them chat through the problem. It was then that Morag decided to withdraw the charges against Roberta because her friend had been through enough problems in her life.

Powers wasn't giving up though. He turned his attention to Jack Reeves. Morag had explained to Powers that Jack tried to get into her bed that night in the apartment. Morag had refused his advances and had gone to her neighbour's apartment, Jake, for help. When she returned, about ten minutes later, she found police storming the apartment.

Powers made the point that Morag had trusted her daughter with two people, Roberta and Jack. Powers claimed that these had been poor judgements of character, and that the choice of people whom she associated with had put her daughter at risk. Although she tried her best to get Powers to see that Jack was devoted to Jasmine and he wouldn't have hurt her it was to no avail. Morag tried to answer the questions calmly and sincerely, but Powers was out to tarnish her. He asked her if she had a drink or substance abuse problem. While she categorically said "no" the fact that he had asked those questions, on record, meant he had suspicions.

The dirty war had truly started.

Relentless questions after questions followed. A poor innocent mother trying to protect her child was nothing more than a lamb to the slaughter. The Chapmans went for the kill at every possible opportunity.

Alcohol figured quite prominently in the probing questions that Powers kept asking Morag. Did she drink spirits, how much wine did she drink, what about Jack Reeves, was he an alcoholic? All those questions kept coming and coming. Powers tried to twist every answer to try and catch Morag out. She held her ground and kept her cool. However, her mind wandered and she eventually lost concentration. She thought about Jasmine, what was she doing, where was she at that time. She thought about Scotland, her home, Forres, what the journey home might be like and her new life after this ordeal was finally over.

But first, she had to continue to endure the onslaught.

Powers wanted Morag to talk about Lawilda and Jimmy Ross. Did she like them? Were they fit to look after Jasmine? Did she trust them? Did they love Jasmine? Did they care for the little girl? With her concentration ebbing, Morag made a mistake.

Powers asked about the hypothetical outcome where the court might decide not to award custody to either Marcus or her. "Where would you want the child to go?" Morag replied that the child would probably have to be taken into care. Powers pounced. "Would you rather she was in foster care or placed with a relative?" Morag replied, "I have no relatives in this state." Powers had made a significant win. He now had it on record that Morag disliked the Chapmans. He could, and surely did, use this to his advantage in court.

If the torrent of questions from Powers hadn't been enough, Neal Pfeiffer, Marcus' attorney, still had his turn.

Again, questions after questions about her relationship with Marcus and about his relationship with Jasmine followed.

Pfeiffer wanted to show Morag in a poor light. Similar to Powers, he questioned her about her drinking habits and about drinking while caring for Jasmine. Morag stood her ground, pointedly telling the attorney that she did not drink excessively. The subject of violence came up.

Morag had stated during those deposition sessions that Marcus had, on several occasions, been violent towards her. "Every other week, he'd either grab me or hit me in some way, or he'd really beat me up, and on three occasions he put a gun to my head."

Unconvinced, or deciding he wasn't making any headway, Pfeiffer turned his attention to Jack Reeves. He claimed that Jack drank too much. He was clearly attempting to show that Morag made associations with "undesirable" people.

During the time that Morag had been giving her deposition, Lawilda and Jimmy Ross had been awarded temporary custody of the child. Since Marcus had repeatedly failed to show up for meetings with the lawyers, a judge had lost his patience and told the court to award Lawilda and Jimmy Ross care of the child for two weeks until the depositions were taken.

I was furious when I found out that Lawilda had won. That's exactly what it had been. She wanted to discredit Morag so that she could get care of my granddaughter. The episode with Jack Reeves just played right into their hands.

So while Morag had to endure all those questions, her little girl was 200 miles away in Woodville with the Chapmans. Each night, sitting alone in her apartment, Morag pondered everything. What would happen if the start of the court case dragged on for months? Would she get Jasmine back or would the court continue with custody to the Chapmans? Morag was becoming more and more depressed. Her mental state was certainly deteriorating, what with the barrage of questions and the unknown about her daughter.

The court had given Morag two days visitation rights to her daughter. When Jasmine saw her mother she kept saying "Mummy, Mummy, can I come home, Mummy? Take me home, Mummy."

Morag rang me and I knew things were turning bad. My poor girl was really distressed. I tried to calm her down and eventually she said "Mum, this is the first time I have had her from the Chapmans and she is crawling around the floor like a baby all over again. She follows me everywhere, and even if I go to the toilet she's banging on the door shouting 'Mummy, Mummy'."

Morag told me that Jasmine was behaving like a pet dog wanting attention and affection. She was really scared for the little girl. At four o'clock that afternoon, to keep the terms of the temporary custody agreement, Morag would have to hand Jasmine back to the Chapmans. The visitation rights did not extend to evenings.

Morag didn't know what to do. She was being torn apart, watching the girl crawling about the floor, a behaviour the girl had got over many months before. It was like Jasmine was reverting to being a baby. The Chapmans had damaged that little girl. Morag screamed down the phone "They are making a fucking mess of Jasmine's life. What do I do?"

All I could think of saying at that time was "Morag, get the fuck out of there with Jasmine."

But where would she go. She didn't have a passport. They had taken that from her when she arrived in Texas. All I knew was that she had to get away. My fear was that Jasmine's love for Morag was being eaten away. I told Morag to go to San Diego, to my son, and her brother, Stuart.

Stuart was living illegally in the US so he probably wouldn't go out of his way to help. But he was our only hope.

I came off the phone and started calling all my horse-owning pals. I knew this was completely wrong, but if I could find a way to get a passport for Morag and Jasmine it might help Morag to escape from the US. If I could find a mother with her daughter on the same passport, we could change Morag and Jasmine's appearance to look like the passport. Frantically, I phoned around loads of people, but I had no luck.

Time was running out. The Chapmans would be calling for Jasmine at 4pm that afternoon.

As the clock ticked away on both sides of the Atlantic, I continued my hunt for a solution.

But it was in Texas that an answer to Morag's problem was being worked out.

Jake Harris, Morag's neighbour, drove her to his ex-wife's house. They stopped outside and Morag sat watching the seconds tick past as Jake went into the house. A few minutes later he returned to the car and handed two passports to her. Caroline was blonde, just like Morag, and Olivia and Jasmine looked similar. I remember Morag telling me afterwards that she took one look at Caroline's passport and told Jake "She looks nothing like me".

Not to be put off by dissimilar looks, Morag coached Jasmine as they drove to San Antonio airport. She told her "Now, we are going to play a little game. I am going to call you Olivia, so if anyone asks you, you must say your name is Olivia. Remember Olivia, the little girl you played with, well, you are going to pretend to be her. Is that okay?"

Kids love games. They don't necessarily have to know why they are playing them, but give a kid make-believe and they are almost certainly up for it. However, Jasmine would have to wait a little longer for the game to start. When they arrived at San Antonio Airport, Jake agreed to buy them a ticket to San Diego. When he went to pay for the tickets he found that his account was a little short of cash. He would need to top it up. They had to go back to Austin and try again tomorrow. This left a further problem. What would Jasmine tell the Chapmans when they picked her up at 4pm?

Morag coached her daughter once again. "Sweetheart," she told the child. "Don't tell anyone that you went to see planes. Just tell them that you went out to see different places. Can you do that?" It seemed that little Jasmine had inherited Morag's strength of character for she simply replied, "Yes, Mummy. Of course I can."

Morag phoned me that evening to update me on the situation. She asked for Stuart's address and I reminded her that he wouldn't help much. He was too caught up with his own life to bother about other people, even his own sister. Stuart was, and still is, a selfish person.

The Chapmans arrived with Jasmine in the morning. "See you at four o'clock," they said.

No fucking chance, thought Morag. She had other plans.

With two airline tickets bought by Jake, Morag and Jasmine took to the sky again, and headed for the west coast of America.

When she arrived in San Diego, Morag called me from Stuart's apartment. After she hung up I thought to myself, oh my God, I have two kids and they are both in America; one of them is an illegal immigrant, and the other one has just become a fugitive.

Life is funny sometimes. Life can be ironic too. Little did I know that I had just sent my daughter off to the very person who, in a few years from then, would battle me in another court, in another country, but for the same reason – selfish greed!

THE WORST SON IN BRITAIN

Life is strange. After the trial in America, I thought that I could rebuild my life. Little did I know that six years later I would be speaking to a journalist from the *Daily Record* in Scotland, telling him that my son, Stuart, would need a JCB digger to drag me out of my house and that I was not going to leave without a huge fight.

I was becoming good at being interviewed by journalists! I have a collection of headlines from the early 2000s, which read:

<display begins>

My son will need a JCB to evict me *Daily Record*

Is this the worst son in Britain? *Daily Express*

The bad son is Britain's worst father as well *Daily Express*

Home, bittersweet home *TV Quick*

<display ends>

Stuart was my first child. Born in 1962, 11 months before Morag, he was always a lively kid. After my divorce from my marriage to Tony Dodds, Morag stayed with her father, while Stuart lived with me in Kingussie. He went to school in Kingussie and had lots of pals. They were forever coming around to the house to play and amuse themselves.

Like me, Stuart was a pretty serious kid. He loved sport and the outdoor life. Swimming, football and golf were his main sports. In fact, he became quite good at golf, making the Grampian Boys Competition and winning some prizes. Similar to other mums, I became his taxi service, driving him to golf competitions in the north-east of Scotland. He won a fairly major competition and was invited to England, to a dinner to accept a prize.

It was about the same time that Stuart went to secondary school that we moved to Forres. I was having problems with my second husband, Donnie Dempster, (but more on that later) and I decided that it would be better for Stuart and me to live in Forres, away from Donnie in Kingussie.

Morag and Stuart never really got on well together. Every time Morag came to visit, the two of them would battle with each other. Maybe it was because Morag had been born too quickly after Stuart; maybe he resented another kid taking the limelight away from him. I think parents should plan a little gap between kids, because I really do believe that children born quickly after each other can have problems with their behaviour in later years.

Morag used to say to me "Why does Stuart hate me so much, Mum?" Years later, Morag still talked to me about Stuart and about their relationship – or lack of it.

Tony Dodds and I were living near Newcastle when I had both kids, about 11 months apart. During the final stages of pregnancy with Morag, I took Stuart to live with my mother, in the north-east of Scotland. I had to go into hospital for ten days, and Tony's mother was not willing to look after Stuart. Stuart was away from me for about two weeks, during which time a new child had arrived. It was probably quite a shock for Stuart to see me with this baby in my arms, suddenly taking all the attention away from him. Maybe that was the start, who knows?

Stuart went on to study at Elgin College. He completed an HNC in Hotel Management and I actually think he really enjoyed his time at college. During the summer holidays, he worked as a waiter at Culloden House and he worked for my cousin who had a restaurant in Elgin. He said that Stuart was a great lad, a hard worker and very pleasant with the customers. Stuart could always turn on the charm, especially when a good-looking woman appeared! I was quite surprised that my cousin and Stuart got on well together because he was a "Gordon Ramsay-type" chef, only the best would do, however, he always had a kind word to say about my son so that was a good thing.

Morag told me a funny story about her and Stuart. They had been at a Christmas party at a chum's flat in Elgin. Stuart had taken a girl from Forres to the party, a farmer's daughter, and had sparked quite a relationship with her. Meanwhile, Morag got a little tired of the party and asked if she could crash out in the flat. Someone showed her to the spare bedroom for the night.

Almost asleep, in one of the two single beds in the room, she suddenly heard voices. That's Stuart, she thought. Oh my God, he is with the girl. Morag very quietly lay while Stuart and his latest girlfriend did the business in the next bed. Morag, realising that the passion had come to an end, spoke out, "Stuart, what time is the bus home in the morning?" You can imagine the shock when he realised that it was his little sister in the next bed.

If nothing else, Stuart had a penchant towards private enterprise. He had an old car that was always running out of petrol. He would go around car parks at night and siphon off petrol from other cars. He almost got caught one night and had to run through most of the housing estates in Forres to escape.

I had started a driving school about the same time as Stuart was at college. I bought a new car and said to Stuart that he could borrow it, instead of driving around in his old banger. One night, I drove his car to Elgin for a service, while he took my new car out for a run with his mates. Unfortunately, I was pulled over by the police because one of the lights was faulty. As I was giving it the old "sorry officer, I didn't realise ..." Stuart cruised past me and gave me a cheeky wave. He was a character.

My brother, Norman, spoiled Stuart, probably because he didn't have kids of his own. Norman had quite a few connections and he managed to get Stuart lined up for an interview with BP, for a steward's job offshore on the oil rigs.

Although Stuart had a healthy income from his work offshore, he didn't have enough for a deposit on a house in Forres. So I gave him some money that I had inherited on the death of my own mother. Also, I was going through a bad time with Donnie so I thought that a refuge would be good for me, just in case I wanted to escape for a while away from Donnie's drinking and temper. Stuart agreed that I could use his place whenever I needed time away.

Things with Donnie went from bad to really bad. Eventually I could not stand living with him. He wanted about £40,000 to buy him out of the home where we lived in Forres. That was a lot of money during the late 1980s. It is hard to believe now, but interest rates at that time reached a record high of 15%, during the Margaret Thatcher years in government. I struggled to get the cash together.

Morag wanted us to buy Donnie out together, but she was struggling as well, and so she couldn't manage to contribute enough to our joint pool of money. My solicitor told me that building societies might not look too favourably on a daughter and mother joint mortgage application. They might think that Morag would eventually get married and ask for her contribution back. My solicitor advised me to approach Stuart and ask for his help. Building societies much preferred a mother and son application. So I asked Stuart for help.

Stuart wanted to get away from the oil rigs. At that time there were no women offshore! Also, because he was a good-looking lad, he was constantly being pestered by gays, especially those in charge of catering services. One bloke used to buy him expensive jumpers and leather jackets. Nice!

So Stuart said, why not sell his place in Forres and use his name to get a mortgage to buy out Donnie Dempster.

Stuart never actually put any cash into the deal; we simply used his name as joint mortgage holder.

It all worked out really well because he got a job with Cunard, on board the *QE2*. He went off for six months, sailing from Southampton to New York, all around the Caribbean, Europe, the Mediterranean and even further afield. He met a girl who also worked on the ship and I remember him calling me, saying "I'm not going to be like my uncle Norman, all alone and sad. I'm going to find a girl and marry."

I remember another call that I got from him. This time the call came from Australia. Stuart commented "Mum, I am now in the same line as you. I just got my heavy goods licence." My boy, always the enterprising type!

Stuart never really settled for very long so it was no surprise that he was off again, but not before fathering a child to the girl from the cruise ship, Dina. She went back home to London to her parents to have the baby. Stuart was not there for the birth. He was off to America, to a ski resort where he sold burgers and coffee.

Morag and I went to London to see the child, my first granddaughter.

I remembered one of the Chapman's attorney's in the custody court asking me "What have you done for your children?" I immediately replied, "I have given them the confidence to get out and see the world, to see how other people around the globe live their lives." That was Stuart. He certainly had the confidence to get out and about. Maybe a little tenacity too.

Confidence is one thing, but too much of it can be bad. Stuart was always confident around women, which got him into trouble on a few occasions. Actually, I don't just have one granddaughter from him; I have two. He had a fling with another girl, a one-night stand that ended in pregnancy. I became a grandmother twice in the same month.

There was an interesting piece in the *Scottish Daily Express* where Stuart's daughter, Rachael, said "My mum has told me all about him as I grew up and I want to meet him, just to ask him why he abandoned us."

Rachael's mum, Tracey, commented in the newspaper "I was 18 when I met him. He came home from the rigs and we'd go out for a drink and then to his house. I called him to tell him I was pregnant and he was quite shocked.

"He called me back and I was shocked at his words. He said 'You have to get rid of it because I have AIDs'.

"The test was terrible – the staff wore masks and gloves, like they were going to catch it from me. I had to wait six weeks for the result and cried myself to sleep every night, believing I was going to die.

"Of course, the test was clear. He didn't have AIDs. It was just an act of evil. He even called my GP trying to find out if I'd carried on with the pregnancy. That's the sort of person he is.

"He liked fast cars. If this was the 1920s, he'd be described as a cad. He can charm the birds off the trees, but he has a wicked temper and a streak of pure evil."

Stuart ended up in San Diego. He didn't have a Green Card so he was effectively an illegal immigrant in America. As enterprising as ever, Stuart started up a little catering business. He would provide catering for outdoor dinner parties. He managed to get into supplying rental cars as well, hiring vintage cars to British people who were travelling across the States.

I went out to San Diego every year to see Stuart. I am not sure how he managed it but I remember once he got the wrong airport. He was supposed to pick me up from my flight but he went to the wrong place! Dozy beggar!

Because he didn't have a Green Card, he couldn't chance trying to leave the US. Immigration would have picked him up, so he just laid low for a few years. However, he ended up in jail. He hit an Irish guy during a bar-room brawl and the Irish guy, knowing that he didn't have a legal right to be living in the US, reported him. Stuart was arrested and put in prison for a night. He had to find a wife, quickly.

He took up with a lesbian soccer player who agreed to marry him so that he could live in the US legally. Stuart automatically got his Green Card, so now he could travel out of the US. And that was when all the trouble really started.

Stuart came over for a visit. I was away from home when he arrived at my house. Not surprisingly, he arrived with another girl by his side, someone from Switzerland who he had met in America.

My solicitor later told me that Stuart visited her during that trip to Scotland. He asked her how he was going to manage to get me out of my home. I had known my solicitor for a few years and trusted her. So when she told me that Stuart had visited her I started thinking about other little niggly things that had happened around that time. I had a barn near to the house and I let it out to a guy who repaired cars. One day, a chap from the council arrived, snooping about, asking about the barn and how it "wasn't being used for agricultural purposes". I had a few caravans as well and another council chap came asking about the use of the caravans. He said "You don't have permission to be letting caravans." Maybe it had been Stuart who had tipped off those people.

After the court case in Texas, I asked Stuart if I could visit him in San Diego, maybe for some company and maybe to tell him about the outcome of the custody battle. He agreed and I went to San Diego for about four weeks.

While I was away in the US, I let out my house to some officers from the RAF. There was an RAF base not very far from my home in Forres so I thought that officers would be quite respectable people who could live in the house and look after it while I was in the US. After all, I wasn't sure how long I would be in Texas so it made sense for me to let out the place.

When I was with Stuart in San Diego, I wrote a letter to the RAF lads, advising them that I was coming home soon and I needed the place back. However, Stuart left America before me and he went to Scotland. Unbeknown to me, he visited the RAF lads and told them that he wanted to re-let the house because he owned half the house and wanted to rent it out. Someone in Forres tipped me off and I called Stuart to say, no, don't rent it out – I want to live there. I was fuming to say the least.

When I came back to Scotland I went to see my solicitor. She told me that I had every right to stay in the house and that nothing could be done to evict me.

The other thing that was terrible was that Stuart had withdrawn all my money from an account that was in our joint names, opened during the time we bought the house. He must have remembered about the account and had gone to the bank and cleared the lot.

I couldn't believe that he had done those things to me. I was in despair. Stressed from the custody case, and now stressed that my son was taking my money and wanting to sell my home.

Right at that time in my life, it all got just a bit too much for me. On reflection, I really don't know why I did it. I guess most people who try to kill themselves can't really give a concrete reason for it.

But I tried.

A few glasses of wine.

A handful of Paracetamol.

A broken woman.

I called a friend and told her "This is it."

Perhaps it was a cry for help. I don't know. But I do know that I would never do that again. Nor would I recommend anyone trying it. Life is precious. It really is.

Even after all that I have been through in my life, I am the first to say that life is so very precious.

Anyway, my chum rushed around to my place, called a doctor, and I had my stomach pumped out. No permanent damage, thank goodness.

One of the doctors at the Elgin psychiatric hospital, where I spent one night, told me "There is nothing wrong with you. It is your children who are wrong. Now, just go home." He was probably right.

After that little episode with the pills and booze, life went quite quiet. I started up a kennels business. A joiner friend built four lovely kennels and the rent from those started coming in nicely.

I have always believed that a rift is a rift and we all have them but we all need to get over them. I knew there must have been a reason behind Stuart acting the way he did.

Probably a woman!

Probably that Swiss girl. Maybe she took a liking to the house when she stayed there. Perhaps she had persuaded him to try and cast me out. So after about a year, I called him and told him that he could come back and stay whenever he wanted to. I wanted to repair the rift and prevent any further damage to our relationship.

He did come back. It was okay, although not as "friendly" as we had been in the past. In fact, I knew things were never going to be the same again.

He left for San Diego and I thought, well, is that it? Will he be back another time? People kept telling me that Stuart would never bother me again. I wasn't too convinced though.

And just before Christmas, as a new millennium was about to start, a court order arrived at my house in Forres.

Another legal fight was about to commence.

MY FIGHT TO KEEP MY BEAUTIFUL HOME

Forres is a gorgeous small town, one of the oldest in Scotland. Located about 30 miles east of Inverness, the town is picturesque and a hub for tourists. It has been a winner of the Scotland in Bloom competition on several occasions and there are many tourist attractions nearby.

The earliest reference to Forres appears in the second century, in a feature written by the Roman traveller, scientist and writer, Claudius Ptolemy. One of his most famous works of literature was a book titled *Geography*, where he wrote about Europe in Roman times. The small settlement of Forres was mentioned in his book.

On 23 June 1496, King James IV of Scotland issued a Royal Charter, which laid down the rights and privileges that the town's people were able to exert over the settlement. This effectively created an important hub on the north-east coast of Scotland.

Sitting between the floodplain of the River Findhorn and the wooded slopes of the Cluny and Sanquhar Hills, the town, with a population of around 20,000, is well known for its award-winning floral sculptures.

Another very famous place near Forres is the village of Findhorn and the Findhorn Foundation. In fact, when Kathy Thomson, Jasmine's appointed guardian *ad litem*, realised that I was from Forres, she was quite excited about the Foundation and had asked me lots of questions about it.

Set up in the early 1960s the Findhorn Foundation is a charitable trust that provides a wide range of residential and non-residential courses in New Age topics. From meditation to living purely from nature's larder, the Foundation has now become known worldwide. Hippies, but hey ho, maybe they have achieved inner peace?

I bought the property and land in Forres because I loved the town and the area around it. I also loved the view from my house. We look across the town and out over the Moray Firth. On a really good day I can see the Black Isle. So with Stuart now back in the US, I had to start thinking about my options and about how I was going to fight the pending court action. I wanted to keep my place in Scotland and I wanted to stop that dirty scoundrel from evicting me. My own inner peace was going to have to wait for a while until I dealt with my thieving son.

One thing in my favour, or so I thought at the time, was the fact that when I built the house, it had gone through the necessary planning process on the basis that it was an "agricultural holding" rather than a house set in 14 acres of land. An agricultural unit wouldn't be as attractive on the housing market as one that was purely listed as a "house".

Through my experiences with the media, I knew how powerful a good relationship with the newspapers could be. The power of journalism was unquestionable so I contacted various publishers, thinking that one or two of them may respond. I was overwhelmed by the media interest in this story.

One of the good things that came out of the press coverage was that someone contacted me, a lady from Elgin. She told me that she had been through a similar situation to my one. Her husband tried to force a sale of their property and land. However, she let the land to someone for more than 12 months and because of this the court had ruled in her favour. The court could not evict a tenant so therefore the ground, and her house, could not be sold.

The letter from the very kind lady in Elgin inspired me. Get a contract, quickly, I thought.

A local farmer, who I knew quite well, agreed to sign a note to say that he was renting the ground for agricultural purposes. I managed to draw up a contract and found a lawyer, outside of the Morayshire area, to represent me. I didn't trust any of the lawyers around Forres because the place is well-known for the Moray Mafia! They all talk to one another so I thought it would be better to find someone who was quite independent from the Moray gang. I was quietly pleased with myself. I cherished the thought of suddenly surprising Stuart and his lawyer with a signed and legal contract that would seriously hamper his efforts to evict me.

The lawyer I found in Inverness was really good. He helped me to employ delaying tactics when Stuart demanded that he be allowed access for valuation purposes. Letters went back and forth for some time. The whole issue played on my mind. I was still in my home but I knew that, someday, probably soon, I would have to face up to the inevitable.

There was a serious outbreak of foot and mouth disease in the country around that time. I used that to my advantage too. I put straw all over the access road and posted signs warning of the dangers of the disease. I put out buckets of disinfectant with brushes for people to wash their shoes and boots before coming onto my land. I knew that the valuation people who Stuart commissioned all liked to dress in their fancy brogue shoes and corduroy trousers, so they might think twice about venturing onto my property. Although it did deter them a little, they were still keen to get access so that Stuart could get an accurate valuation.

The farmer who leased the land from me was shooting rabbits one day when a guy from the local estate agency arrived. The chap said "Is that gun for me?" The old farmer simply fired some shots at the rabbits, missing them completely. He was usually drunk and I doubt if he could have hit a 16-ton truck, never mind a local estate agent. Nor a rabbit for that matter.

At least the ground that I owned was rising in value. A property developer came to visit me and offered to buy out my "tenant" and to pay my son off. I refused, thinking that maybe the day would come when I really had to take the offer. But for now, I was intent on fighting Stuart all the way.

Eventually, the civil action that Stuart had raised was heard in Elgin Sheriff court, on 3 September 2004. The day after the case, the *Daily Express* ran a long feature.

<display begins>

A devastated woman has been forced out of her home of 21 years by her own son. Former horse breeder Flora Dempster now faces the grim prospect of life in a caravan overlooking the house in which she hoped to spend her retirement.

Flora needed her bachelor son Stuart Dodds, 42, to act as guarantor when she bought her 14-acre croft from her ex-husband after their divorce 21 years ago.

Mr Dodds paid part of the £400-per-month mortgage for just five months before leaving for a new life in America, where he set up a vintage car hire business and a catering company.

Flora said: "I have struggled to pay the mortgage ever since by myself. It is my home. But the law is on his side because his name is on the title deeds.

"My son is despicable. I never thought he'd stoop to using his own mother.

"He knows he will be left a lot of money in his father's will, but he can't wait for us to die, he wants it now."

The house in Morayshire will go on the market next week. Mr Dodds stands to gain at least £70,000 from the sale of the house.

<display ends>

I had no choice but to settle. Stuart and I sat with the lawyers for a whole day, facing each other over a table in the court. I decided then that I never wanted to see him again. I really did feel that he was despicable.

The final paragraphs of the feature in the *Daily Express* read:

<display begins>

Flora added: "The house was going to be my pension. Now I might have to try and find work at my age."

Mr Dodds, thought to be staying in Scotland until the house is sold, refused to comment.

<display ends>

So I had to endure all those people coming to the house to view it. There were many prospective buyers and finally the house was sold. I ended up giving Stuart £110,000.

Actually, things turned out quite nicely in the end. The people who bought the house allowed me to remain in the place until I built a new one, which was positioned about 100 yards further up the hill. The new house, which is where I live today, has even better views across the town and the front side of the house was built mostly using glass. So the combination of stunning views and the sun-trap because of the glass makes the house absolutely ideal. I named the house Callaly, but more about that later.

In all of this mess with Stuart, I really felt sorry for Rachael, Stuart's daughter (the one-night stand in Elgin). She had spotted the various articles in the newspapers and had contacted me. She said that she wanted to meet her father and that this would be a good opportunity because he would be travelling to Scotland a lot to deal with the case.

I had to go to Inverness to discuss things with the Land Court, because I had tried to convince the lawyers that it was agricultural land. Rachael wanted to come with me to Inverness because Stuart would be there too.

Rachael was a good kid. She was 15. There really wasn't much in common between us so our relationship never got off the ground. But she did come to Inverness with me.

I briefly saw Stuart at the court in Inverness. I tried to get him on his own so that we could get the whole issue of the property sorted out without taking it further. Alas, not to be. Stuart went to the toilet and Rachael spotted him so followed behind.

A chill still runs down my back when I think back to that scene. Rachael collared him in the corridor and, with a nice, friendly and cheerful smile, said "Hi Stuart, I'm your daughter." All he could muster from that soulless mind of his was "I know who you are" and walked straight past her.

Poor Rachael was devastated.

ON THE RUN

What makes the debacle with Stuart and the house all the more tragic was that he started his quest to evict me only a few years after I got back to Scotland from Texas. I think that riled me more than anything. Morag and I had gone through an awful lot during the custody case, only to find my son now adding to the stress by pursuing his greed.

One thing I did learn about all of this was that I am a "control" type of person. When Stuart battled with me over the sale of the house, I was partially in control of the situation. I was here, at home in Scotland, so I was able to exert some degree of influence. I handled the whole thing really well, and I think it was because I could make things happen as I was familiar with my surroundings and the people involved. In contrast to that, of course, was the uncontrollable situation I faced with Morag when she went on the run in San Diego. I had no control, I was thousands of miles away from her and Jasmine, and I was worried sick.

Morag and Jasmine landed in California at lunchtime and they went straight to the address I had given her for Stuart's apartment. I remember Stuart telling me about a person he had rented a room from, and I thought he would probably have a key for Stuart's apartment. So Morag phoned this chap, only to be informed by him that Stuart had already been in contact and told him not to help Morag if she called. The guy told Morag that Stuart knew about the federal warrant for her arrest. Morag was stunned. How could her brother do this to her? More importantly, how did

Stuart know all of this? Morag firmly believed that it had been Marcus who tipped Stuart off about the arrest and about her being "on the run".

Morag told me a little story about Jasmine when they came out from the airport terminal in San Diego. Jasmine suddenly shouted "Look mummy, there's Granny." I can't imagine what Morag was thinking at that time. It was impossible for Lawilda to have made the journey from Austin to San Diego quicker than Morag, but her mind was in turmoil so she panicked when she heard her daughter's exclamations. However, not to worry, it was a Lincoln the same colour as Jimmy Ross's car that Jasmine had spotted.

Morag and Jasmine set out in a taxi for Stuart's flat. The woman who looked after the apartments answered the door and Morag explained that she and Jasmine had made a surprise trip to visit her brother and the little girl's uncle. The woman was wonderful to Morag and she took a liking to Jasmine. She used her master key to let them into his apartment.

Morag called me from Stuart's place. She seemed fine. "I'm safe here, mum, so don't worry," was what she said to me. But, I did worry, because I got a call from Stuart not long after Morag called me. "She's in my flat, using my phone," Stuart shouted. "Do you know that she failed six drug tests and that she has crossed the border so the FBI are on the case?" I calmly told Stuart that Morag hadn't failed any drug tests, that was a lie Marcus had concocted to get Stuart to turn Morag away. I was furious with Marcus for doing such a thing. I was also furious with Stuart for not taking his sister's side and for not helping her. He was only interested in protecting himself. He probably knew that Morag, being on the run with a warrant out for her arrest, would bring the police and FBI snooping around. Stuart was an illegal in the US so he didn't want any trouble. Marcus had warned him that helping a person on the run could lead to a jail sentence of five or six years. Stuart was probably frightened by this.

Stuart told Morag that she could stay one night and that was all. Morag phoned me again and, in tears, told me that Stuart didn't care about her and that he told her and Jasmine to get out in the morning. Where would she go? I was sick with worry for her and Jasmine.

Of course, back in Austin the trouble had really started. When the Chapmans came to pick up Jasmine and found her missing, they immediately spoke with Jake Harris. He confirmed that he had taken Morag and the girl to the airport, but he told the Chapmans that Morag and Jasmine were bound for Britain, not San Diego.

Morag told me later that she found out Marcus had phoned Stuart after they discovered Jasmine was missing. He kept asking Stuart "Are they with you?" At least Stuart did the right thing by telling Marcus that he had not seen her. However, after coming off the telephone to Marcus he told Morag to leave.

Morag packed her things and took off with Jasmine. Walking down the road pushing the buggy with Jasmine inside, Morag had no idea where to go. Cast out by her brother, in a city she didn't know and on the run from the FBI, she would have been forgiven for just bursting into fits of despair. However, she kept strong. She passed a garage where a man spotted her. Morag told him that she was looking for a refuge so he ordered a cab and told her where she could find some people who would look after her.

Back at home, I was frantically trying to think of a way to get her out of the US. The border between the states and Canada can be quite lax so I thought if I could find her a passport maybe she could get a bus into Canada.

I had quite a lot of friends and associates from the liveries. A lot of young girls had horses so I phoned around and asked if anyone had a passport for a child. I tried everything. I even tried Dina because her daughter to Stuart

69

would have been about the same age as Jasmine. I wrote to Dina but she never got back to me. Perhaps she didn't want to get involved.

Back in the US, Morag found a refuge for battered women. She told me later that the first few nights and days there were horrendous. Young women would lift their dresses so that they could show their scars and marks left by aggressive and violent husbands or lovers. Morag took badly to her stay at the refuge. She spent most of the time in tears and in despair. A small break came when the people who ran the place told Morag that they had organised a room at a nearby facility run by the Salvation Army. So, on 30 November 1994, Morag and Jasmine moved into their little room.

Every day, residents at the Salvation Army centre had to vacate their rooms for two hours so that cleaners could get to work. Actually, there was another reason. Staff at the centre used this time to thoroughly search each room for drugs. All they found in Morag's room were clothes and Jasmine's cuddly toys.

Morag would walk the streets of San Diego every day so that her room could be "tidied". Fearful that they would be spotted, Morag tried to keep a low profile. However, it was not easy for a mother of a little child to remain incognito, even in a large and busy city. But relentlessly, Morag protected her child and complied with the rules of the centre. She wandered around the local parks, keeping one eye on Jasmine while another was kept on the lookout for police or maybe even private detectives.

In fact, an investigator had been employed by the San Diego County Department of the Public Defender to trace Morag and Jasmine. The Chapmans had probably painted a nasty image of Morag to the authorities so they were no doubt trying to find a young woman who was high on drugs and out of her skull on alcohol. It is ironic but weeks later the investigator was asked to submit a report of his findings.

He presented a statement from Ms Cooper Jones, an official at the Salvation Army shelter. In contrast to the image likely portrayed by the Chapmans, Ms Jones said

<display begins>

Ms Dodds seemed like a caring mother, although she was quite distressed by her situation. The child was well cared for. Jasmine wore clean clothes and her hygiene was good. The child's hair was a little dishevelled but she seemed well taken care of and clean. Ms Dodds was attentive and responsible as a mother.

Ms Dodds was very concerned that there were enough towels so that she could bathe her child. Although she was very distressed during her stay at the centre, she was still able to look after her daughter.

Ms Jones stated: I never saw Ms Dodds drinking at all nor had I seen her under the influence of drugs. Ms Dodds was a caring and fit mother.

<display ends>

As Morag looked after her daughter, the federal machine ramped up a few gears. The FBI instructed its agents to notify airports, railway stations and bus depots to be on the lookout for a young woman and a small child.

Morag called me a few times and I hurt along with her. Regardless of the physical distance between us, I felt for every tear that she shed. One consolation was her obvious excitement when she talked about Randy Berry. She was clearly in love with him and she missed him terribly. I could tell from her voice that she was deeply infatuated with the man and I secretly hoped that it would work out between them. However, she had other things to worry about at that time. How to get out of her present dire situation in San Diego.

A lucky break came one day when she was sitting on a park bench, crying, with little Jasmine beside her. Suddenly, Morag heard a man with a very definite Scots accent ask her "What's wrong?" Almost without hesitation Morag poured out her story, probably more with relief that someone would listen to her desperate situation.

Sam Frazier, a former professor from Dundee, listened intently to Morag as she told him about her plight. Of course, she didn't let out every detail, enough to let Sam know about her despair but not enough to raise any suspicions about calling the police.

Sam lived alone in a nice house in the city. He had a spare room, a garden that was well tended and he was in need of a cleaner. He immediately offered Morag the job as cleaner, telling her that the spare room was large enough for Jasmine to share it too.

So, in December of that year, Morag and Jasmine moved in with Sam at his house in Kantor Street, a nice part of San Diego that overlooks the San Clemente Park. The park is a beautiful place to take kids, and it is lined with ancient walls that contain fossils from 45 million years ago. Morag loved to take Jasmine to the park where she could roam freely. The park, with its closed-in valley, offered at least some degree of privacy for Morag and Jasmine.

Morag tidied up Sam's apartment, and she felt quite secure at his place. Sam was good to Morag. He didn't pry too much, nor did Morag offer too much detail of her plight. I think Sam probably knew Morag would, in her own time, tell him about her troubles. However, time was, as always, running out for her.

Morag had asked Sam about getting passports. He had told her that the nearest Consulate-General was in Los Angeles, about 80 miles north of San Diego. Sam said that anyone turning up at the office and saying they had been robbed and their passports had been stolen would surely get sorted out with new passports. Morag held that thought in her mind.

Sam employed a gardener, a Mexican called Thomas Garcia. Tommy, as he told Morag to call him, fancied his chances with her and would make unwanted advances.

Unbeknown to Sam, the Mexican's relentless approaches to Morag were starting to get to her. One night, Tommy started singing a Mexican love song, which he thought would woo the gorgeous Scottish lass into his bed. Morag had other ideas. She grabbed a kitchen knife and, holding it in front of him, exclaimed "If you come near me again you'll get this. I'll stick this in you." Riled, the Mexican stormed off. But soon he would return.

Morag picked out a book from Sam's well-stocked bookcase. It was *A Christmas Carol*, which was very apt for the time of year. Of course, the story is about a young child who is given a chance, hope and happiness. The tale is about a bitter old miser, Ebenezer Scrooge, and his transformation resulting from supernatural visits. Published in early Victorian Britain, the book transports the reader through stages of misery, sadness and, at times, little hope for the future. However, through the thought-provoking supernatural visits, the main character is transformed. The plot interweaves desolate children with capitalism in what was a difficult era in British history. Perhaps there were messages to Morag from the tale of Scrooge. Maybe capitalism, in the form of the Chapmans, could be overcome, if love, dedication and courage existed. Morag had plenty of love, she was totally dedicated to Jasmine, and she had buckets full of courage. It was time to act.

Morag told Sam "Jasmine and I have to go somewhere. It should only take a couple of days, but there is a chance that we might not be back."

And so Morag and Jasmine took a coach from San Diego up to Los Angeles. The journey took a few hours but time seemed to race past quickly for her. She had to come up with a plausible story to tell the British Consulate. She could hardly walk into the building, go up to reception and say, I am Morag Dodds, on the run from the FBI, and here is my kidnapped daughter, Jasmine, who is being pursued by her temporary guardians, Lawilda and Jimmy Ross Chapman. No, she needed a better cover than that!

Morag and Jasmine walked from the bus depot to the British Consulate's office. They walked past shoppers intent on buying their kids the latest Christmas-craze toys and gadgets. They walked past street sellers, flogging their cheap and cheerful wares. And they walked past white-bearded Santas who smiled and hollered at the mums and kids. But no stopping for Morag. No presents to buy, no cheerful riposte. And no cheerful souls at the Consulate either. She waited with Jasmine beside a huge Christmas tree that had a train running around its base. A dour security guard told her to "Get that child away from the tree" because he didn't want her touching it. When Morag told me that story I thought, what a prick. So much for the season to be jolly, cheerful and kind to kids.

Another really laughable thing was the woman who eventually met with Morag. She told me later that the woman asked Morag why she was there. Morag, deciding honesty was, in the end, a better option, spilled out everything that had happened to her and Jasmine. The woman went somewhere but returned a few minutes later. She said to Morag "Did you know there is a warrant out for your arrest and a lot of people are looking for you?" Morag told her that was why she was at the Consulate's office, to get some help. And then the woman said "Well, I'm sorry, but we're all off to a Christmas lunch. Can you come back tomorrow?"

Unbelievable.

Morag told me that she just sat down and cried. Trying desperately to hide her discomfort from Jasmine, it was all getting too much for my daughter. She said that she simply didn't know where to go to spend the night. Morag thought, while everyone went out to their Christmas parties, she and Jasmine would be sleeping on the streets.

A break did come for Morag, in the form of a kindly receptionist at the Consulate's office. Spotting Morag with her daughter, he came over and asked what the problem was. He told her that he would organise a taxi and book a hotel for the night. Although Morag tried to explain that she had no money to pay for a taxi let alone a hotel, the receptionist didn't seemed too perturbed. He simply took some money out of his pocket and told her that it was for the taxi and for a hotel.

While Morag was in Los Angeles, I kept imagining a call coming from her. I thought perhaps the call would come from LA International Airport, from my daughter as she waited, with two passports, to board a plane travelling to Britain. I kept hoping that the Consulate would help her and would be able to get "replacement" passports for them both. I guessed that LA was about 12 hours flying time from Britain, and a short hop from Heathrow in London would take her back up to Scotland. I kept trying to believe that my two girls would be home within 24 hours, maybe 48 at the most. Instead, in the morning, Morag packed her bag and headed straight back to the bus depot. She wasn't chancing any more help from the British Consulate.

Morag called me from Sam's house in San Diego. What a terrible state she was in. She kept saying "They are going to take Jasmine from me. We'll have to start all over again. Mum, what am I going to do?"

Morag was right. The police would soon be coming for her. All thanks to the Mexican gardener. Apparently, and I only found out about this much later, Tommy Garcia had searched through Morag's things while she was out of the house. He had discovered Marcus' phone number. The Mexican was intrigued by this foreign girl and her little daughter. What was her story? Why were they in San Diego? Why didn't she say an awful lot about her circumstances? He was intrigued enough to call Marcus.

With Christmas only six days away, Sam and Morag enjoyed a little quiet time on the patio outside Sam's house. Morag had been sitting there enjoying the thought that she was safe, at least for the time being. Thinking about her home in Scotland, and the life that she thought would eventually come back, she smiled at the memories of her childhood family Christmases. Presents, warm fires burning, snow falling in Aviemore, all conjured up a warm and cosy feeling.

Suddenly, two police officers appeared around the side of the building in San Diego. Morag's worst fears were about to be realised. They grabbed her arm, pushed her face-down, handcuffed her and marched her off to one of two police cars that had been dispatched to Sam's address. Jasmine was taken into the other car.

Morag was taken into the local police station and was told by the police that they were going to contact their colleagues in Austin to arrange for her to be transported across states. She was put into a prison cell while they sorted out what to do next. Meanwhile, Jasmine had been taken to a care centre, awaiting transport back to Austin too. Morag had little doubt that Jasmine would be handed over to the Chapmans and given custody once again. Little did she know at that time, but the Chapmans would be given extended custody, until the start of the trial in mid-February.

I ENTERED THE BATTLE AND
HEADED FOR THE US

The news about Morag's capture had been relayed to Randy Berry in Austin. Randy called me with the news that I was dreading. He told me Morag had been arrested and was in prison in San Diego. He said that she was being transferred to Austin but that might take a few days. One other thing that he said to me that really concerned me was in relation to the Chapmans.

Randy told me that it looked as though Lawilda and Jimmy Ross were abandoning their idea of getting the court to appoint Marcus with custody of Jasmine. Instead, they were gearing up to get full custody themselves. Randy told me that I should get myself over to Austin so that at least another plausible person for custody could be presented to the court.

On Christmas Day, I rang the detention centre where they were holding Morag. The guards there refused to put the call through.

Morag was allowed one call, providing it was a call within the US. She called Woodville and asked to speak to Jasmine.

A few years later, David Leslie, a journalist with the *News of the World*, wrote a book about Morag's custody battle. He interviewed Morag about her struggles to get custody and about her time in prison in San Diego. In his book, Leslie quotes Morag as saying

I hadn't spoken with Jasmine for six days and wanted to wish her a happy Christmas. The phone was answered by Lawilda, and I said, 'Can I speak to Jasmine, please? I want to wish her a Happy Christmas and to tell her her mummy loves her'. But Lawilda just said, "I don't know what you hope to gain from this. She is outside playing with the dog, and she cannot come to the telephone." The other girls at the detention centre were waiting to find out what happened and what Jasmine had said, and when I told them about the conversation they just said that Lawilda was an evil bitch.

Stuart made no effort to visit me while I was in prison, and I didn't hear from him. No doubt he was scared in case the US Government got to hear. But an elderly lady, a Scot living in California who got to hear about me when the case began to be reported in the local newspapers around San Diego, turned up to visit. She said that she felt great sympathy for me and had been so moved by reading how I had gone on the run with Jasmine that every time she thought about us she started to cry. She had gone to great lengths to find a store that sold British goods and had brought me a tartan-coloured tin of Walkers shortbread. It was such a lovely gesture that I cried when she left. A complete stranger had gone to a lot of effort to bring me a little piece of home.

<display ends>

Morag was right. A complete stranger had made extraordinary efforts to visit her in prison, while her own flesh and blood, in the form of Stuart Dodds, hadn't even bothered to contact her. Even her own partner, Marcus, had failed to call her. And as for Lawilda, well, refusing to let Jasmine talk to her own mother on Christmas Day was shocking beyond belief.

Back at home in Scotland, I stirred things up a little by contacting the *P&J*. On 26 December the front page of the newspaper ran a feature "Snatch Mum in US Prison Nightmare".

A young north-east mother spent Christmas in an American prison cell after a desperate bid to win back her daughter in a custody battle.

Ms Dodds (29) is in a women's prison in San Diego, California, charged with abducting her two-year-old daughter Jasmine.

The former Forres Academy pupil – a qualified nursery nurse who worked in Aberdeen – was even refused permission yesterday to accept a long-distance Christmas Day telephone call from her frantic mother back home in Forres.

<display ends>

Randy Berry was quoted in the newspaper

<display begins>

Under Texas law, Morag is in serious trouble. A judge has granted temporary custody of Jasmine to the parental grandparents. In the circumstances, with the child's parents being unmarried, this is acceptable under Texas law. That is why Mrs Dempster has to enter the lawsuit.

Morag is being held, pending an extradition hearing on the 30 December.

<display ends>

I was quoted in the newspaper feature as saying

<display begins>

This past week has been a nightmare. How can anyone keep a mother from being with her baby daughter especially at Christmas time? Morag must be heartbroken, and I can't even get to speak to her on the telephone. It just does not bear thinking about. I only wish I had gone out to America earlier to give her moral support. She has been driven too far, and I am obviously concerned for her mental state. Now it appears that the only way my daughter will see her child again is if I raise an action for custody. Under Texas law, I have the right to do this.

I couldn't have been more serious. I needed to get out there.

There was another concern too. Tony Dodds, Morag's father, had received a letter at his house, which was addressed to Morag. Tony called me and told me that it was from the local hospital. Apparently, Morag had had a routine ovarian cancer check carried out which revealed she might have a serious infection. I immediately called the detention centre in San Diego and told them that Morag needed an urgent examination. I told them that I would personally hold the guards responsible if anything happened to Morag if they failed to get the tests done. My direct approach to the people there must have worked, because Morag did get her examination and, thankfully, all was clear.

It was one of those funny situations. Morag told me later that she had been sitting in her cell one minute and then the next she was lying on an examination table with her legs up in the air, all because "My mother had made a call from Forres in Scotland to a prison in San Diego." How completely bizarre was that?

Randy's final words to me on the phone really convinced me that I needed to go out to Texas. He said "Let's work this case around you getting custody. The court will not look favourably on Morag getting sole custody because she had broken the court law by going on the run. The best chance we have is to get you over here and to go for maternal grandparent custody."

Back in California, the extradition order had been signed by the relevant judges. Morag's transfer had been set for 9 January 1995. Two officers were sent from Austin to escort her back. They handcuffed her to one of the seats in the aircraft but she vehemently objected, threatening to scream and yell the whole way if they didn't release her. Reluctantly, the officers agreed to do so, but one of her arms was cuffed to the escort officer. Morag thought to herself, well, if this plane does crash, at least you are coming with me.

Morag was put in prison, on the abduction charge, when she arrived back in Austin. She spent three days there, while waiting for a preliminary trial to be arranged to work out what the authorities were going to do with her.

In his book, Leslie asked Morag how she felt about going back to Austin. She said

<display begins>

I appeared in court, and by then I was in a terrible state, worrying whether I'd ever see Jasmine again. I was in such turmoil that I didn't even know what happened at the hearing until it was all over and someone explained the proceedings to me.

<display ends>

What upset Morag more than anything was the sight of Marcus in the court room. He was with a blonde-haired female. In the book, Morag said

<display begins>

I thought, all is lost here, when I saw them together. I've got absolutely no chance. I'd come from jail at the end of a line of people all in shackles, and the first thing I saw was Marcus cuddling a blonde woman!

<display ends>

The "blonde woman" was actually the District Attorney! She was the one who had called me to tell me that Morag was in San Diego, on the run. I told her that Morag had little choice but to take her child away from those people in Texas who were trying to dictate what should and what shouldn't be done with Jasmine. I reminded her that the British court had made it a condition that Morag would not be separated from her child while in the US. Yet, here was Morag, her child taken from her by the Chapmans. What else could she have done but run. I don't think that blonde attorney saw it my way though.

I was lucky because I made it to that preliminary hearing, so I could see the state she was in and I could start to make sense of all this stuff that was going on. My trip out to the US was eventful as well. I had looked at all the flights from San Diego to Austin and tried to anticipate which one Morag was on. I thought it might be nice for me to arrive in Austin early so that I could go to the airport and see Morag arriving from California.

I remember sitting in the arrivals lounge at Austin watching and waiting for the flight from San Diego to get in. People were hanging bluebells from the ceiling at the airport. Bluebells, or bluebonnets as they are called in Texas, begin to appear in fields from March onwards. They are the "flower of the state" and it is tradition that people stop alongside the road so their kids can carefully walk through the fields of flowers to have their picture taken, surrounded by the sea of blue colour. Texans call it "baby in the bluebonnets". Since it was only January, I thought they were hanging bluebonnets early. Maybe they had been plastic ones!

Although the colourful flowers, plastic or not, were very pretty, I wasn't distracted too long from my mission. Fight for everything you have, is all that I was concerned about as I watched the blue flowers being suspended from the airport ceiling. I was more preoccupied with watching for planes coming in from the west coast.

Unbeknown to me, Morag's flight hadn't come directly into Austin from San Diego. Instead, they had taken a different route, so I had missed her arrival. While I had been watching the ceiling of the airport terminal changing from a drab airport-ceiling colour to a bright blue, Morag had arrived, been taken to prison, had been searched several times and told to change from her blue prison clothes into orange coveralls.

Randy had organised an attorney to represent Morag on the so-called abduction case, a chap called Ken Houp. We met him on the Sunday morning. Ken opened his office so that we could discuss the case with him. He called the judge who was going to hear the case on Monday and told him that Flora Dempster was over in the US and that she would look after Morag until the formal trial could get underway. Ken Houp was amazing. He seemed to be chatting to the judge as though they were arranging a game of golf, rather than talking about releasing a person from prison.

I walked into court on the Monday morning, hoping that by the end of the day Morag and I would be leaving the court room together. However, although the judge had agreed with me being there to support my daughter, she decided to set bail as well, about £2,000. The circuit judge on duty that day, a female, had decided to impose bail because Morag had talked to a journalist from the daily Austin newspaper. The judge did not like this at all, so she decided to punish her by setting bail.

I talked with Alastair Bisset from the *Press & Journal* in Aberdeen and he in turn talked to his editor. The people at the newspaper agreed to put up the bail money, providing they got it back. So back into court we went, but now with the bail money secured. My heart bled when I saw Morag coming into the court room that second time. There was a long line of guys, all around six feet tall, shackled by their arms and feet. At the end of the line of prisoners was my Morag, all five foot of her, chained to the men in front. All of this because Marcus and his vindictive family had taken a dislike to her. Chained together with murderers and rapists, for what, abducting her own child? Talk about Americans using a sledgehammer to crack a nut!

Eventually, the court decided that Morag could be released, pending the custody trial and then, following the outcome of that, the abduction case. They released her into my custody but not before fitting a clamp to her ankle. We had to get an apartment and we had to arrange for a phone to get connected. Morag had to go back to prison for one night so that I could get those things sorted out.

Randy Berry fired a warning shot to us. He said that the Chapmans would drag the case out. He told us that their tactics would be to try and wear us down, so that eventually I would give up and go home. No chance. They obviously didn't bank on Scottish resolve. I was sticking by my daughter and she was in turn sticking by her own child. I kept focusing on my flight home, but not a flight for one. Three tickets to Scotland was firmly my goal. So Lawilda and Jimmy Ross, you can bring it on.

I met a lovely lady called May Cherry. Originally from Aberdeen, May had read about the case in the Austin newspapers. She wanted to help so she got in contact with us. Morag and I were renting a small apartment that had little in the way of utensils. May Cherry wanted to visit and I was a little embarrassed by the fact that we had only two cups. Not to be put off at all, May arrived with a whole load of stuff, including cups, teapots, cutlery, cooking pots and all sorts of other necessary items for cooking.

It is quite amazing to think that, while there are terrible people in the world, who are vindictive and completely heartless, there are others who put themselves out to help. May fell into the latter category. She heard about our plight, and she immediately wanted to help. We should always remember that no matter how we feel about those who have fought us, there are always those who are willing to befriend us.

So, Morag and I spent about six weeks in that little apartment in Red River Street, Austin, patiently waiting for the custody case to commence. Well, I say patiently but that is perhaps not the way it should be described. Although Morag had to attend numerous depositions and other meetings, she was effectively under house arrest so she couldn't go out. I tried to go out a few times but it was difficult walking around Austin doing the window-shopping thing while in the back of my mind was a pending court hearing and, more importantly, an unknown decision.

The landlord of the apartment brought a single bed for me, which fitted under the stairs in the kitchen/lounge area.

May Cherry invited me to one of her meetings at the "Scots in Austin". In fact, Morag and I were both invited to a Burns Supper, so Morag asked her contact at the court if she could leave the apartment, which would mean breaking the house-arrest order that had been imposed on her. The court officer asked why she wanted to go out to the Scots in Austin, and I remember Morag having this conversation on the phone with the woman. Morag said "It's a Burns Supper" to which the woman replied "A what?" Clearly, Burns is not celebrated by everyone in Texas!

They wouldn't let Morag go to the meetings at Scots in Austin so I went with May. The meetings were quite good. It was surprising how many Scottish people were out there. I didn't say very much; May did all the talking. It was a little embarrassing in some ways because May organised a collection for Morag and I, so that we could buy groceries and other essential things for our apartment. Although I didn't really want to take their money, I had no idea how long we would be in Texas so I guess the money did come in handy. It was very kind of them to give us some cash. May was considerate and very friendly.

I had become something of a celebrity at the Scots in Austin meetings. I met another lovely woman there, Christine Matyear. Christine, a lecturer at the University of Texas in Austin, had associated immediately with Morag's plight. She told David Leslie for his book "I was very taken with the story, since I had been the subject of a custody battle when I was about three or four myself.

"It was similar in some respects – grandparents versus my father following the death of my mother. I was very young, but I remember the anxiety of being separated from my beloved parents.

"In light of this emotional response, I felt very sympathetic towards Jasmine and began following the developments of the case. Morag had been under a great deal of stress and was largely without resources. I think that hearts went out to her from many people in Austin because of that. It was her passionate concern for little Jasmine that won me over. When she spoke about her, the maternal distress showed very plainly."

With Morag out of prison we now had the challenge of getting an attorney to fight the custody case. Terry Weeks had no hesitation, I think because he was really fascinated by the Scots girl who had given so much to fight for her child. However, we did have a problem. Terry, like all attorneys, had to pay for the food on his table. His fee was going to be about $10,000. We simply did not have the money. Marcus had failed to provide for Morag, as he was instructed to do. Morag had been cleaned out, because the trip to the US had been expensive. I was running out of funds as well, nearing my credit limit on my cards. The trip to Texas, the apartment in Red River Street, and our on-going costs were all mounting up. I did think about selling one of my horses and a trailer, just to cover the cost of food. Luckily, a knight in shining armour, in the form of Jasmine's godfather, helped out.

Jack Reeves took a call from Morag, who told him about the legal fees that needed to be paid. Jack told her that he would call back in a few days and to stop worrying. I thought, easy for you, Jack. Both Morag and I were sick with worry. How long was this going to take, how many weeks would the Chapmans drag this out, putting us through hell? Give him his due, Jack phoned back two days later and said to Morag "Go hire that attorney, the money is yours."

Jack had gone to the bank manager of his local branch and asked for £7,000. Of course, the bank manager asked him why he needed the money and Jack told him all about the case. Perhaps the manager had already seen the press coverage, in any case, he agreed to give Jack the loan.

I remember sitting in Terry's office for the first meeting. Randy and Morag were both there too. Terry bombarded her with question after question, not surprisingly. Randy was intently listening to the exchange of information between Terry and Morag. I looked at Randy and knew immediately that he had feelings for Morag. Just the way he looked at her and smiled. I think he was besotted. Randy was married to a woman called Kathleen, but they had split up. I only found out this much later but apparently Kathleen, who went to live with another man, came to Randy and asked him to take her back because it hadn't worked out too well with her lover. Randy agreed but they lived quite separate lives although in the same house. It was good to know this because many people blamed Morag for Randy's separation from Kathleen when, in fact, he had been having marital problems long before Morag came onto the scene.

I think Morag had definite feelings for Randy too. However, she was angry and she made sure that her anger focused her. She had been badly treated by the whole American legal machine and she wanted to focus now on getting her daughter back. A new love in her life, although welcomed, was not something that she needed at that time. She needed to concentrate, keep as calm as possible, meet the Chapman family head on and win back Jasmine. A love affair with a man very much came second in her life at that time.

Morag and I kept thinking about Jasmine. What was the little girl thinking? A break came when Randy managed to get the court to allow me to see Jasmine, about the end of January. Morag was delighted, at least one of us could see the girl and find out how she was coping with being away from her mum.

I was given permission to meet Jasmine at a local park in Austin. Morag gave me a Barbie doll to give to her daughter. Morag sprayed the doll with her perfume so that Jasmine would recognise the scent of her mummy. It was bizarre though. Randy took me to the park but he stayed in his car. There was Lawilda, Jimmy Ross, the guardian *ad litem*, a security guard, me and, of course, Jasmine. The Americans certainly know how to over-react.

Jasmine looked depressed, certainly not the little cheerful girl that I had last seen in Scotland. I told her that her mummy loved her and would see her very soon. Her little eyes lit up as I said those words. She was very tearful during those 30 minutes in the park. All the while, we were watched by the Chapmans and their entourage. There was a little burn running through the park and I so much wanted to march Lawilda over to that burn and throw her in! How could she put a little child through this much stress?

I took some photographs of Jasmine, and Randy drove me to a place where they did instant developing. I wanted Morag to see her child, but when I saw those photographs come out of the machine, of Jasmine crying while being pushed on a swing, I really wondered whether or not to give them to Morag. Instead of showing a happy-go-lucky wee Scottish girl, they showed almost a total stranger. White-faced, distressed, worried, anxious are all words that I can think to describe my granddaughter. They had cut her hair too. She had refused to let them brush her hair so Lawilda decided to cut off her beautiful curls.

When I showed Morag the photographs she went to her room in the apartment in Red River

Street and burst out crying. I wondered if she would ever come out again.

MY DEPOSITION

The long wait in the apartment at Red River Street continued. The authorities gave Morag a little slack in terms of deactivating her clamp for a few hours each day, so that she could attend meetings with her attorneys and give her deposition.

Some days, time went past really quickly. Some, in fact many, days dragged. When would the case start, how would the jury take to Morag, how was Jasmine getting on? So many questions.

It was my turn to give a deposition. Having never done this before, I was a little apprehensive.

It was 2pm on 31 January 1995. I was seated at the desk in the law offices of William Powers, Lawilda and Jimmy Ross' attorney. Randy Berry was there too, together with the official court Certified Shorthand Reporter, Debbra Wood.

The session on that afternoon started off with the formalities, called "written stipulations". These are made under the rules and regulations that govern court proceedings in the State of Texas; *Texas Rules of Civil Procedure Rule 206*. It was a little daunting for me to watch the attorneys go about their business, but it was all quite laid back. When asked whether or not each person agreed to the "stipulations" my representative said "Yeah, I'm Randy Berry representing Flora Dempster and I've read and agree to those stipulations."

The usual stuff was asked. Name, address and where I was staying in Texas. Powers' next question was a little strange though. He asked me to describe my permanent residence. I explained that I lived in a three-bedroom house that had been built about ten years ago on 16 acres of land in Forres, Scotland. I also added that the house had a stable block. I hadn't realised that this would get so much attention. Powers asked "Did I understand you to say a 'stable block'?." I then had to describe "for the record" what a stable block was. Ten minutes into the deposition and I was really wondering if life would ever be the same again! It took ten minutes to give them my address, so how long was this going to take in total?

Next came my relationships. Oh dear, I thought.

"Mr Don Evans, is he your partner in life, or is he your partner in business?"

"Do you have plans to marry Mr Evans?"

"Are you living together?"

"Where do you live?"

"What do you work at?"

"How much do you earn?"

I wondered where all of this was going. So many questions about me. I felt like saying to Powers "Actually, I think you will find that the court case is about Jasmine." However, I guess he was trying to establish whether or not I was a "fit" person to be seriously contemplating taking legal custody of the girl. I tried to keep as calm as possible and I gave concise answers to all of his questions. Randy Berry sat quietly next to me as the questions kept coming.

"Does Scotland have its own currency?"

"Is it the same value as the English pound?"

What?

"No," I replied. "We use the English currency, and yes, it is the same value as the English pound."

There was a brief interlude when someone came into the room and handed Powers a document. He then showed me the document, which he called Exhibit Number One. It was my CV. Powers asked me to confirm that this CV was a true reflection of my academic and work history. He also reminded me that, in the US, a deposition was taken under oath and had the same status as if the answers were taken in a court. I nodded. He then reminded me that, for the purposes of the record, a verbal answer was needed to each question. "Can we agree to do that?" he asked.

"Are you familiar with the American educational system?"

I think my glib reply upset him when I said "Well, you can try me."

"I don't want to try you. If you are not familiar with the system I don't want you guessing. I want to get as close to equivalent as I can, so I will tell you about the system."

Oh dear, I thought.

"From the ages of approximately five to 18, children in this county are in public school and the last four years of that, from about 14 to 18, we call High School and that is really where public education ends and then you can go on to college or university from there."

Nice.

"So tell me. I see from your CV that you went to Keith Grammar School."

Sure did.

I then had to explain about the Scottish system and that primary school was first, followed by secondary and then, maybe, but not in my case, higher education.

Powers went on to ask about my first marriage, to Tony Dodds, Morag's father. A bizarre exchange of questions and answers then took place. I couldn't remember exactly when I had married Tony so Powers got more and more confused. It was like a sketch from a comedy show on television.

"What was your first husband's name?"

"Anthony Dodds."

"What was the period of time that you were married to Mr Dodds?"

"About seven years."

"Okay. So if you married him in 1964, you were probably divorced around 1971?"

"I was married to him before that."

"Ah, so this 1964 marriage would be your second marriage?"

"No. That was the first one."

"I don't understand. Do you know when you got married? Mr Berry, can you calculate from the first child's birth?"

"He is 32."

"All right. How long before Stuart was born had you been married?"

"A year."

"So if we went back 33 years that would be about 1961."

"That's correct."

I was glad we had sorted that one out. It was almost an hour into the deposition and it felt like a lifetime.

Powers asked about Tony, his job and then about his illness. Of course, my divorce was the next thing up for questioning and, following that, my marriage to Donny Dempster. Then came some stuff about my drinking habits and whether or not I had ever been treated for drinking problems. Then he asked if I had ever consulted with a health professional for a mental health problem.

Finally, we got on to the subject of Jasmine.

I explained to the attorney that Jasmine had been born in Aberdeen, at the local hospital. He asked a load of questions about the location of the hospital in relation to Forres, so I explained that Aberdeen was about 80 miles east of Forres. I told him that I was in Greece, on holiday, when she was born but that I had phoned every day to find out about Morag and Jasmine. As soon as I arrived back in Scotland I went to the hospital to see them both. He then asked a ton of questions about how many visits I had made to the hospital, how long Morag had spent there before getting home and how many visits I made after she returned to Forres. I could now start to imagine what Morag went through with her depositions. I'm only the grandmother and I felt as though I was getting the third-degree.

Powers moved over to a white board on the wall and began writing years and months. He said "So, for a six-month period of time you had some regular contact with Jasmine. Can you remember if she moved to Newcastle before Christmas of 1992?" My head was buzzing with seeing all those dates on the board. "Okay, so we celebrate Thanksgiving, do you have a similar holiday to Thanksgiving?" "No," I said. "We have something called the Potato Holiday!" A strange look appeared upon his face! In fact, I think a strange look appeared on all their faces. Maybe they don't pick potatoes in Texas.

"Does that happen in November?"

"No, October."

"Okay, so did Morag and Jasmine leave Scotland for Newcastle before or after the Potato Holiday?"

More dates and more years appeared on the board. I couldn't think straight.

Then he moved on to Morag and Jasmine leaving for Austin, and more dates were written onto the board. Before long, Jasmine's life had been mapped out on that little white board in Powers' office. I knew exactly what he was trying to do. He was trying to present a case that showed I had little contact with Jasmine. However, I wasn't giving in to this. Lawilda and Jimmy Ross had had far less contact with her than I ever did, so I stood my ground and tried to present an image that showed I knew Jasmine well, which I think I did.

With the board plastered in something that looked like calculations needed to take a spaceship to Mars, Randy Berry asked "Can we break for a coffee?"

After coffee, the questions continued.

Powers asked about Stuart and Morag when they were kids. Who did they live with? How long did they live together as kids? When did Morag come back to stay with me after she left her father's place? On and on it went.

Then came a "curve-ball" as they say in the US.

"Did you ever hear that Morag had been sexually abused by the man who was living with your mother?"

I knew where this line of questioning was going. I tried to think ahead and predict what was coming. I told him that it didn't revolve around my mother, but Tony's stepfather. Stuart and Morag used to visit Tony's mother, their grandmother, who married a guy called George Adams. When Stuart was seven he went on holiday to Spain with his grandmother and George Adams. The following year he refused to go back on holiday with them. At the time I didn't think too much about it, perhaps it was just down to growing pains and Stuart maybe not wanting to holiday with the older folk. However, about two years later, he spilled out the story. Adams had sexually abused him.

I called the police immediately and they contacted the local office where Tony's mother and Adams were living. George Adams admitted to the offence and was charged. When Morag and I were in Austin she told me that she had also been abused by George Adams.

Powers went on to talk about Morag and about the years after she left school. She had taken up with a man called Malcolm Steele, who she lived with for about four years. After Malcolm, Morag married Donald Ross.

"Did you like Donald Ross?" asked William Powers.

"No, I did not. He was dour."

"I'm sorry. What is the word?"

I guess they don't use the word "dour" in Texas.

I really didn't like Donald because he was dour, sullen and quite withdrawn. A strange choice, I thought, for a lively and extroverted girl like Morag. But they do say opposites attract. He had a temper too. One night I had to drive over to Morag's place because Donald had been very nasty to her. She was tearful and very upset.

"After Donald, who was next in her life?" asked Powers.

Well, that had been Marcus. Powers glanced over that one. "Next?" he asked quickly.

And now for Jack Reeves. Powers asked me if I knew a man by that name. I explained that he was Jasmine's godfather. A few questions were asked about Jack.

Randy Berry spoke up again. "Can we have another break?"

The minutes and hours ticked past.

"Ms Dempster, you have intervened in this lawsuit asking for custody of Jasmine. Would you tell me and tell the court why you think you should have custody of Jasmine at this time?"

My reply was simple. I said "Because she is a Scottish child, she was born in Scotland, and I think she should come back and stay in her own country with her mother. I have a three-bedroom house, so they can both come back and stay with me until Morag gets settled again."

Powers, with pen in hand, was back in front of the white board. "Let me rank the preferences for what a jury might do in this case."

I felt uncomfortable at this so I conferred with Randy, but Powers was in full flow with his marker pen.

"Assuming the court has four options, Morag, you, Marcus and the paternal grandparents. If you were deciding, who would be the first person to get custody?"

I went through with his little game of "pick the right parent". I told him that Morag should be first choice and then I should be in second place. I put Marcus as number four. Powers then asked about visitation rights and how often I thought that Marcus and the Chapmans should have access to Jasmine. In America? In Scotland? How often? At Christmas? This was all just speculation and hypothetical but I knew there was a good reason for Powers dwelling on this. He would raise all of this in court.

San Diego came up next. Powers asked about my involvement with Morag going to California with Jasmine. I kept my replies brief and very much to the point. He asked about the abduction charges so I said that, because we didn't have such charges in Scotland, I was unaware of how it worked in the US.

Tommy Garcia, the gardener, was mentioned by Powers but I said that I didn't know anyone of that name. Sam's name came up too, but again I said that I had no idea who he was, which was true, because it was only after Morag and I met up in Austin that she told me the whole story about the lecturer and the Mexican.

More hypothetical stuff came up.

"Ms Dempster, suppose the court were to award custody of Jasmine to you, what kind of access should Morag have?" I replied "Total access." There was no reason in my mind why Morag should not get complete and unconditional access to her child. With the next question, I could see where Powers was heading.

"Would you describe to me what you know about your daughter's drinking habits?"

"Morag has stayed with me since she was 13, so I know what her drinking habits are."

"What are they?"

"She likes occasional wine, drinks wine most of the time when she does have a drink. Perhaps a couple of glasses in an evening."

"Has she ever had a problem with alcohol?"

"No."

"Did Morag tell you that, when Jack Reeves was visiting her and the police arrested him, he was intoxicated on that evening?"

Oh, dear, Jack Reeves again.

"Did Morag tell you that she was intoxicated that evening?"

"She wasn't intoxicated that evening," I replied.

He asked a few more questions about Jack Reeves and about Morag's drinking habits. Then he moved on.

He asked about my trips out to Austin and about my relationship with Lawilda and Jimmy Ross. They had both been okay with me. They were quiet-living people and seemed friendly enough. I had gone out to Austin one Christmas and had visited the Chapmans. They had a beautiful house in Woodville and a large area of ground.

I visited Morag in Woodville when she was pregnant with Jasmine, and I stayed at her house. One night a bad argument got up between her and Marcus. He had gone out with Stuart, who was also visiting, and had spent a night on the town in Austin. Marcus never came home that night. He arrived home the next evening, which was when the argument started. Morag was complaining that she had been left for long periods on her own while Marcus went off somewhere. To stop her yelling at him, Marcus decided to put Morag into a hotel that night, but she did not want to go. He physically lifted her out of the house and tried to manhandle her into the pickup truck. Morag ran to the outside of my bedroom window and started banging on it. What could I do? I was a guest in someone else's home. It was up to my hosts to sort out troubles in their family. Arguments happen. This one, I thought, could have turned really nasty though.

"Did Lawilda or Jimmy Ross act badly towards Morag?" Powers asked.

"Lawilda did to Morag."

"How did Lawilda act badly?"

"An argument got up between them."

"What was the argument about?"

"Morag had been describing what Marcus was like back in Scotland. Lawilda came out with a nasty statement."

Marcus often let his temper get out of hand, he was often very violent and uncontrolled at times.

"What did she say?"

"Lawilda upset Morag by saying that she was going to take their child away when it was born."

Enduring those hours of questions was energy-sapping, but I kept going because I was determined to do everything within my power to stop Lawilda taking my granddaughter away from us. Finally, Powers declared an end to the deposition.

Thank goodness. I just hoped that I had done enough.

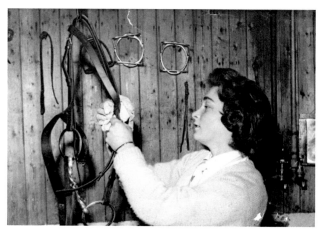

Top: Flora and new-born Jasmine at Aberdeen Hospital
Bottom: Flora at Callaly Kennels

Top: Tony and Flora's wedding in Aberdeen
Bottom: Flora riding horse Sarah

JANE HOTSPUR'S
COLUMN

Flora works in hunt kennels—and she loves her job

THE winds screamed across the aptly named High House, Callaly, home of the West Percy Foxhounds, on the day I went to see Flora Simpson, one of the few girls employed in hunt kennels in the North of England.

There was a good fire in the tack room, whose work shelter, having first paid her respects to the three horses which are Flora's special charge.

MAIN JOB

In her second season at the Kennels, Flora's main job is to look after the horses, and to give a hand with the hounds if necessary.

"I know most of the hounds by name, except a few of the white bitches," she told me. "When the boss issues most near the Kennels I help to look to the meet," she went on.

Her day starts at 7 o'clock with the clean chores of mucking out and exercising the horses before breakfast, after which comes grooming. My first stop the holiday is over and the races scrubbed it is almost time.

"In the afternoon I get the tack ready for hunting, and then see the horses are right for the night. Some afternoons I help the huntsman to walk out the hounds," she said.

HOT BATH!

On a hunting day the coach, she has come home, before backing over to the meet, usually playing out all day and hunting hard. "Then all I want to do is get into a hot bath and fall into bed," she added. Not surprising, really.

Flora began working with horses at a busy trekking centre at Cruickshields, near Southend. "We had about 20 gunmen, and used to trek every day," she told me. From Scotland Cruickshields, her home is in Keith, Banffshire; she went to Gloucester, where she had three polo ponies to look after.

"We did a lot of travelling, often to Windsor or Cowdray Park. While I was in Gloucester I went to Badminton—we were nearly washed away, but I enjoyed every minute.

After Gloucester she went home to Keith, where she took a job in a shop. "I just couldn't stand an indoor life, and soon left to find another job out of doors. That's when I came to Northumberland," she said.

Although she hadn't done it, she would like to work with point-to-point and show jumping horses, if the opportunity ever arises.

During the summer she plays tennis, and whenever she can she goes to Salisbury for a game in the evening. She likes dancing and knitting as her other interests, but after she had looked after her small flat and cooked her meals, there isn't a lot of time to indulge them.

AT CRUFT'S

OFTEN at weekends, when I take my favourite walk from Charlton to Fawberry Cottage, I meet a string of Border terriers out for exercise.

They are from the kennels of Mrs. Phyllis Mulcaster, of Clavering Cottage, Charlton, who has just returned from Cruft's, where she has had some success with her show bench.

Her show bench is a beautiful dog, and as the surrounding dog show, and was second in the next probably, and third in the minor limit and open classes. In the hall these classes he was entered.

She had the prefix "Portholme" from a piece of land.

At present she has 12 adults and two litters of puppies in the kennels, which are descendants of that first bitch. "The Border is a completely unknown Border breed of terrier, which is becoming quite popular in America, and I have sent about 50 across the Atlantic," she added.

She took the prefix "Portholme" from a piece of land

near Huntingdon, where she lived. "It is a large tract of land, without a tree or shrub, and completely surrounded by water—actually an island island—where I used to exercise the dogs," she explained.

APPOINTMENT

A NEW appointment for Mrs. W. Epton Lloyd, wife of the Vicar of Alnwick, has been announced by the Ministry of Pensions. She has become a member of the Northern Gas Consultative Council.

Mrs. Lloyd is a member of numerous charitable committees, in Alnwick, and is a governor at the Duchess's School.

She was responsible for restarting the Alnwick Citizens WVS, which had ceased to function after the war, and has been Centre Organiser since 1954.

Mr. and Mrs. Lloyd came to live in Alnwick just before the end of the war.

Part of 13-year-old Flora Simpson's job is to keep the saddlery clean.

NEW WOMAN INSPECTOR APPOINTED

A FAMILY tradition of police service, which started in Bristol many years ago is being continued in Northumberland by the appointment which became effective last week.

In Cyprus

During her seven she has attended police courses in Northumberland and Hampshire, as well as a short course abroad. She had a two year stint with a Panasonic (Cyprus) Police Division.

She was promoted sergeant in 1953 and in her present rank this month. Her father served for 18 years with the Bristol City Police Force.

Miss Hunt's predecessor has been seconded to the Uganda Prison Service.

Miss Joan Muriel Hunt, to succeed Miss Marjorie Garnett as Woman Police Inspector.

Thirty-two-year-old Inspector

RECORD HALF-YEAR FOR CO-OPERATIVE BAKERY

AT the first half-yearly meeting of the Coparmdale Co-operative Bakery at Amble last Thursday the chairman, Mr. J. Tayler (managing secretary), Widdrington Society) presided and Mr. W. O. Hardy (manager) and Mr. K. H. Scott (secretary) were also present. Representatives from the federal societies of Amble, Broomhill, Berwick and Widdrington attended.

Opening the meeting the chairman said "There are two very pleasing items here to me to draw your attention to. Firstly that for the first time in five years we register a record increase in sales.

"After making an allowance for a 27-week half-year, the sales show a substantial increase over these realised in December, 1961. In 1960 and the following years trade steadily declined until December last when it began to show an improvement, to the short year that fall has been reversed and our previous loss exceeded.

Heartening gap

"A very heartening sign is the increase in sales which is shown by the catering activity of the society and their popularity for weddings and similar functions increases opportunity wherever we wish.

"Secondly," I am able to recommend a dividend to members of 10d. in the £. an increase of 1d. on a year ago and an increase of 4d. on two years ago. This, in spite of alarming increases in expenses due to wage rates, shorter hours and various forms of welfare. In addition, your discount of 30 per cent. remains at this substantial level."

Second to none

In moving the adoption, Mr. A. Robinson (chairman, Amble Co-operative Society) stated that their bakery and bakery products were things that members could be rightly proud of as they were second to none. Discussing members' reasons he realised that by the manner in which they purchased these goods in ever-increasing quantities from their local societies.

Mr. W. O. Hardy seconded the motion and the meeting unanimously carried it.

The balance sheet showed a gross sales increase over the corresponding period of £3,300, bringing the annual turnover to £70,973; expenses increase of £578 to £8,671, including a wage increase of £700, and net trading surplus increase of £269 to £1,537.

Guild talk on Widdrington

There was a good attendance at the weekly meeting of the Women's Co-operative Guild, Widdrington, on Thursday when Mrs. E. Queen spoke on the A.B.C. of dividend. Discussion followed and the meeting was thanked by Mrs. J. Todd, seconded by Mrs. E. Hindmarsh. Officials elected for 1962 are:—President, Mrs. E. Queen; vice-president, Mrs. J. Hollandl secretary, Mrs. S. Smith; committee, Mrs. Todd, Mrs. Trench.

A CHILD'S PETTICOAT, KNICKERS

THIS sweet little underwear looks wonderful in a floral silk, crépe or crepe. Plain colours are equally delightful when edged with lace.

There are three patterns given. Pattern is No. XIII and sizes are also months, 12 months and three years. Material required: Two yards of 36-inch material.

Full directions for making up, together with diagram, will

Farm fare cookery
By Margaret Alden

Legion women at Wooler

There was a good attendance of the monthly meeting of the Wooler British Legion's section held in Headquarters on Tuesday evening.

SEMOLINA SOUFFLE

MILK of excellent quality is not just a seasonal food. It is available in as more easily

Top: Jasmine in Texas aged two
Bottom: Morag, Jasmine and Pip the pony

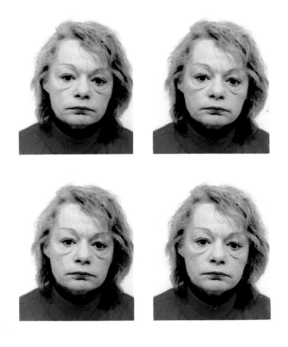

Last photographs taken of Morag, 2008

Top: Morag's resting place, Spey Kingussie
Bottom: The Macdonald family at Delgarvan Farm, Banffshire, Scotland.

Top: Dalgarven Farm, Mary Park, Banffshire
Bottom: Flora's grandmother Elizabeth Macdonald in 1907

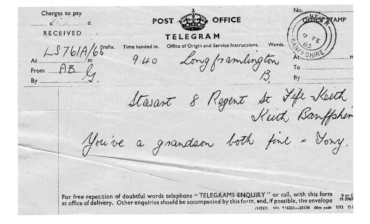

Top: Morag at a dance in Dallas, Scotland
Bottom: A telegram announcing Stuart's birth.

THE EARLY YEARS AND A PLACE CALLED CALLALY

At times of stress and upset, I think we all look back on our lives, to our childhood days when the only thing that stressed us was going back to school after the weekend.

My earliest memories of my childhood undoubtedly revolved around horses, which played, and still do play, a very important part in my life.

I remember my grandmother, who had a farm called Dalgarvan Farm, in Ballindalloch. The small settlement of Ballindalloch, located mid-way between Grantown-on-Spey and Craigellachie, is more famous for its castle than anything else.

Billed as the Pearl of the North, Ballindalloch Castle is one of the most romantic and renowned castles in Scotland. Located right in the heart of Scotland's whisky region, it is one of the few private castles in Scotland and has been in the Macpherson-Grant family since it was erected in about 1546. The castle has a wonderful collection of 17th-century Spanish paintings and boasts that it has one of the finest collections of art in the country. The grand dining room with its magnificent fireplace, the vaulted hall and the cheerful nursery with its collection of antique toys, make the castle a great place to visit.

I vaguely remember Granny taking me to look at Ballindalloch a few times, and we had picnics in the wonderful grounds and gardens there. However, I don't really remember a lot about her. I often reflected on this during the custody case, thinking that Jasmine won't remember me either if she has to live in the US.

I lived in Fife Keith in Banffshire, with my mother. My father had an affair with someone else so I don't have much recollection of him being around. Apparently, my mother found a letter in his pocket from a woman he had met while in the army. That was enough for her so, when I was a baby, my mother threw him out of the house. I think he saw me once, when I was born. We didn't talk about him, even when I was growing up his name was never mentioned in the house.

Fife Keith is now part of the town of Keith, a lovely picturesque centre in Speyside. Fife Keith, originally built by the Earl of Fife, was located directly across from the old town of Keith. The Earl decided that he wanted to compete with the town of Keith, which was why he built up the land across from his rival town. Nowadays, Fife Keith has merged with the old town, together with the newer parts of the settlement, to become what is known as the town of Keith. There is a wonderful bridge right in the centre of the sprawling town, which was built by mourning parents after their child was lost while trying to cross the River Isla. The town is home to the famous Strathisla Distillery.

My mother was a strong woman. I guess she had to be, bringing up my brother, Norman, and me. There was a six-year age gap between us, which is possibly why we never really got on. In fact, I remember my mother talking about Morag and Stuart, saying "It's like the same thing another generation on" referring to how Stuart had behaved with Morag, just like Norman did with me.

We lived in a large house in Fife Keith. My mother took in lodgers, to help pay for the necessities of bringing up two kids, so there were always men around our place. We would often go to her parents' farm, where she organised shooting outings for her lodgers. My brother learned to shoot there.

Although she was a very strong person, she would always send me to the shops to complain about stuff. The "mince was too fatty" or the "butteries were too salty", I used to say to the shopkeepers. I grew up tough!

Fife Keith introduced me to another half of society. We didn't have much money, so no new clothes or new toys. We had to make do with old things that were around the house. We had to make our own fun. In contrast to my meagre childhood, the Laidlaws, who lived across the street, had everything. Irvine Alan Stewart Laidlaw, was the son of Robert Laidlaw, founder of the woollen mill in Keith. Irvine Laidlaw went on to become a member of the House of Lords, and he was listed in the *Sunday Times Rich List 2012* as the 105th wealthiest person in the UK, with a fortune estimated at £745 million.

I remember when the snow fell in Keith. All the kids went out onto the street on their sledges. I, of course, had an old heavy sledge that had been made by one of the lodgers, while Irvine Laidlaw had a smart state-of-the-art machine. Many years later, Irvine was featured in a newspaper, for helping young people in Keith. He put up lots of money to help youngsters get started in their careers. I wrote to him and told him that I was glad to hear that he'd done well and that he was helping the young people of the town. I added a little piece in my letter to him about the sledge. "Did you remember my old sledge? I seem to recall that you had a really light one that could be steered." He wrote back to me and said how nice it was to hear from me. He added "The sledge came from Canada as a present!" He went off to boarding school so I didn't see much of him during our later years at school.

My love of horses started from a very young age. An ice-cream seller used to trudge the streets of Keith, with an old Clydesdale horse pulling a cart. I used to run along with them as they sold the ice-cream, often getting to help undo the horse at the end of the day. The local butcher in Keith had a trotter racehorse. I pleaded with the owner to let me walk the horse after races, during its cool-down session. I loved doing that. I would rush straight from school so that I wouldn't miss the chance to take the horse out for its stroll along the Keith Show racetrack.

I managed to get a part-time job with trekking ponies at a place in Craigellachie, which was seven miles from my home. I loved going out with the ponies on long treks around the gorgeous scenery of Speyside. A friend of mine, Jill, who I'm still in contact with, said to me "You're not going to learn anything here with these ponies, you need to go south, there is lots of money and there is lots of stuff to learn." I looked through the *Horse and Hound* magazines and spotted an advert for a "helping hand" at stables in Gloucestershire that looked after polo ponies. I wrote a letter to the lady, and included a reference from Jill. The lady had once had a Scottish cook so she thought we were all wonderful people north of the border. I got the job.

My mother wasn't too pleased at the prospect of me going off on my own, especially because I was only 16. Gloucestershire? Where was that? I had never been further than Aberdeen, some 50 miles away, so I had no idea where on earth that place was. I remember looking it up on a map, thinking it was so far away that it would take a week to get there. In fact, it did take me quite some time to travel to the stables. I left Keith at three o'clock in the afternoon and finally arrived in Gloucestershire at 12 o'clock the next day. My mother wanted me to travel via Birmingham so that I wouldn't have to use the underground in London, resulting in my journey taking about 10 different trains.

Working with the polo ponies provided great experience for me. These animals were well looked after and well cared for. The woman had an ex-racehorse that was to be retrained as a polo pony, but I wasn't allowed to ride it. One day, when the family went away for the day, I was given the task of "walking" the racehorse to the stable block, at four o'clock. No problem, I thought. So, I went up to this massive horse, with only a head collar, no bit or anything else. Walking the horse would be fun, but jumping on and riding it back would be much better fun!

So, I climbed onto a nearby fence and jumped onto the horse's back. Well, it started to trot.

Then, it started to gallop.

By the time I was alongside the house, the horse was at full pelt, and there was no way that I was going to be able to stop the beast. I remember passing a washing line, thinking, will I jump off? No, better not.

In a flash of a second, both horse and me went straight into a cul-de-sac where the stables were. Obviously the horse knew where it was going. In the middle of the block of stables was a garage and the horse ran straight into one of the doors, which was closed! It fell onto its side, and I simply stepped off its back.

I looked at the concrete and saw marks where the horse's shoes had dug into the cement. The horse seemed to be okay, and I was able to walk it into its stable.

The family came home a little while later. I watched them walking across to the stable block, thinking that I had better pack my bags because I would be sent on the first train back to Scotland. I spotted them looking at the concrete. "What happened?" the woman asked me. I told her that the horse just pulled away from me and that I couldn't stop it. "Okay," she said. "Next time, put a bridle on it when you are picking it up." Wow, the horse got away with it, and so had I.

I returned to Keith after six months in Gloucestershire, for the winter months. I worked in a chemist shop and then headed away again. This time, to Northumberland, to work with fox-hunters.

The place I went to in Northumberland will forever be indelibly marked on my brain. It was called Callaly, and I had such a wonderful time there. So much so that I named my present house, Callaly.

The kennel huntsman at Callaly was well into his sixties so he certainly needed help with the hunt. I worked as the groom at the kennels, mainly working with the whipper-in who is the person at the rear of the hunt and who makes sure the hounds keep up with the huntsman at the front of the pack. Within a very short time I was promoted to whipper-in. I reckon I was the first woman in Britain to be appointed in this position because it was mainly men who did the whipper-in job. Known as the Jewel of the North, the West Percy Hunt takes place around the Cheviot Hills and runs through spectacular scenery and countryside. Established in 1897, it was disbanded during the Great War and was re-established again in 1919.

The *Northumberland Gazette* ran a feature about me. A journalist called Jane Hotspur wrote a regular column for the newspaper. She interviewed me and on 16 February 1962 her column read

<display begins>

The winds screamed across the aptly named High House, Callaly, home of the West Percy Foxhounds, on the day I went to see Flora Simpson, one of the few girls employed in hunt kennels in the North of England.

There was a good fire in the tack room, where we chatted, having first paid my respects to the three horses which are Flora's special charge.

In her second season at the Kennels, Flora's main job is to look after the horses, and to give a hand with the hounds if necessary.

"I know most of the hounds by name, except a few of the white bitches," she told me. "When the hunt meets near the Kennels, I help to hack to the meet," she went on.

Her day starts at 7 o'clock with the usual chores of mucking out and exercising the horses before breakfast, after which comes grooming. By the time the bedding is done and the yards scrubbed it is dinner-time.

"In the afternoon I get the tack ready for hunting, then see the horses are right for the night. Some afternoons I help the huntsman to walk out the hounds," she said.

On a hunting day she exercises the horses, before hacking over to the meet, usually staying out all day and then hacking back. "Then all I want to do is get into a hot bath and fall into bed," she added. Not surprising, really.

Flora began working with horses at a pony trekking centre in Craigellachie, in Scotland. "We had about 20 garrons, and used to trek every day," she told me. From Scotland she went to Gloucester, where she had three polo ponies to look after.

"We did a lot of travelling, often to Windsor or Cowdray Park. While I was in Gloucester, I went to Badminton – we were nearly washed away, but I enjoyed it all the same."

During the summer she plays tennis, and whenever she can she goes to Rothbury for a game in the evening. She lists dancing and knitting as her other interests, but after she has looked after her small flat and cooked her meals, there isn't a lot of time to indulge them.

<display ends>

I was about 18 when I went to Callaly Hunt.

As a youngster, I was fired up with enthusiasm and motivation. I had been working with trekking ponies, polo ponies, and now hunting horses. I fancied trying, maybe, show jumping next. I was keen to learn, loving working with these beautiful animals, and thoroughly enjoying life.

Tony asked me one evening "Would you like to marry? If you will, that would be great. If not, I will buy a mini-van." I told him to buy the mini-van.

But I fell pregnant, which changed a lot for me.

I met Tony Dodds when I was at Callaly. He was working on a farm nearby and I met him at a local dance. It was young love. Tony and I eventually married. His father, Arthur Dodds, was a great character, and I loved sitting talking with him for hours on end. I think it was Tony's father who inspired me to get into business, because he made a small fortune with his bakery business and on stocks and shares. They moved house once and found hundreds of pounds stashed under floorboards of the old house. I remember Tony's granny wanted to buy a Yorkshire Terrier puppy. They looked for money and found a bag full of half-crowns, about £25 worth, which was a lot of money back then. The coins were rusty so Tony's mother had to sandpaper them to get rid of the rust and dirt. There was money everywhere!

Tony and I married in Aberdeen, but we went back to Northumberland to live, at a place called Longframlington. Tony was overjoyed at the thought of me being pregnant. I think his life as a kid had been difficult, because there was a big age-gap between his mother and father, so they never really enjoyed a "happy family life". Tony wanted to make up for what he had missed out on – he wanted a nice family environment for his wife and kids.

My mother visited us at the cottage. Tony was excited because he had just delivered a calf so I left him telling my mother all about the delivery. I went off to a local sewing class. However, my world started to cave in when I returned home. My mother said "It's Tony. He is in a bad way." I rushed upstairs to find him looking terrible. He had lost feeling in his legs. I ran to the local pub and asked to use their phone. The GP came out straight away and examined my husband. Paralysis had moved from his legs into his arms and chest. He couldn't move. The doctor made a series of calls and, before I had time to think, Tony had been taken to hospital in Newcastle.

Tests after tests were carried out, while I waited for news. Eventually, the doctor told me to expect it to be bad. Blood vessels in his spine had burst, causing blood to leak into his spinal cord. An immediate operation was going to be performed. He might never walk again. Worse, he might not make it through the very difficult operation.

Tony was 23. I was 19, and maybe about to become a widow.

Fear not, the operation worked. Although it was going to be a long road to recovery, Tony would live and he would be able to walk, eventually. Spurred on by the birth of our first child, Stuart, Tony bounced back. We went to live near his parents' house. They provided us with a large deposit for a two-bedroom house in West Allotment, near Newcastle. Within two months of Stuart being born, I was pregnant again.

It was nice in that house in Northumberland. It was like Coronation Street, a row of back-to-back brick houses. All the neighbours talked to each other and we had a lovely time there.

Tony was on benefits mostly, but he did eventually get a job driving for a garage. He did a bit of wheeling and dealing too. He loved going to auctions and he would buy all sorts of furniture and then sell it later. We saved to pay our electricity bill, and Tony would buy stuff at auction rather than use the money to pay the electricity company. "We'll get cut off," I kept telling him. "Nae, it will be okay," was his usual response. It usually did come okay because he would sell the stuff for a better price than he paid for it.

Arthur, Tony's dad, was becoming quite ill around about that time. Tony's mother took him to Madeira for the winter months because he couldn't cope with the snow and frost in England. The poor chap was going blind. He would always bring back presents for us and the kids. A lovely old fellow was Arthur Dodds. He had a great business head, unlike some other people in his family.

I wondered why the blood clot in Tony's spine had burst. He had had a previous accident while working on the farm and I thought perhaps it was something to do with that. He had lacerated some tendons in his hand so I thought maybe a blood clot had formed and spread down his back. However, the doctors at the hospital told us that Tony's condition was hereditary. Many years later I still think about his illness. If it is, like the doctors said, hereditary, then Morag and Stuart may have the same condition, something waiting to erupt at some stage in their lives. Jasmine too, may also have it. One of my many reasons for writing this book is to pass as much of my family history on to Jasmine, so that she can learn about her past. Perhaps she will be able to get her spine checked to see if she has inherited a potentially life-changing condition.

Although Tony was making good progress, he needed to find a new job. Farming was completely out of the question for him after the illness. Tony and I discussed all our options and, somewhere during the long and in-depth analysis of our situation came an idea. We waved goodbye to our home in England and headed north, to Kingussie, in Speyside, south of Inverness. We bought a large stone-built house that had nine bedrooms and three bathrooms.

Tony got a job as a part-time driver and he had a second job working in a local bar. Tourism was developing nicely in this part of Scotland, what with the skiing in the Cairngorms and with the new centre that was being built in Aviemore. We started a bed and breakfast, which was an instant success.

The kids had a great time at Kingussie. They each had their own room and there was always plenty of people coming and going. We filled the bed and breakfast rooms almost to capacity all the time, so that meant money was coming in nicely. The kids grew up with the freedom to roam and to explore.

It wasn't all good news though. We were told by a friend that a woman in the village had been gossiping about our bed and breakfast, and how it was "lowering the tone" of the village. We were offering a night's accommodation at about 15 shillings, which was considered too cheap by some people. Tony decided to confront the woman, leaving her in no doubt as to his thoughts on the subject.

When I look back, I do so with fond memories of Kingussie. Well, almost. There was just a little niggle in the back of my mind.

When Tony worked on the farm in Longframlington, we became friends with a local family. We used to go to their house once a week, for a bath. The chap offered to take me out on driving lessons which, without hesitation, Tony agreed to. While I was out learning to drive, Tony was left behind with the lady of the house. During his time in hospital, I guess he had a lot to think about. Perhaps people who are preparing for the worst moment of their lives think about everything that has happened. Perhaps that is the time we try to repent our sins? Anyway, as I sat alongside his hospital bed, he said "Don't stay with me, because I don't deserve you." What a strange thing for him to say, I thought.

And then it all came out.

While I had been learning to drive, Tony and our lady friend had been having sex. Tony had decided to confess all of this to me while he was waiting for news of his illness. So, not only was I pregnant, I had a husband who was maybe never going to walk again, and who had just told me that he had been unfaithful to me.

I cried all the way back to the bus after that visit to the hospital.

From that moment on I never trusted Tony not to do the same thing again.

THE GOOD AND THE NOT-SO-GOOD IN SPEYSIDE

Our first few years in the village of Kingussie were really quite wonderful. Our business was growing nicely, money was coming in, and the kids had a great time. We were a proper family. We had some fun too. We bought geese but that wasn't a success. We then moved on to rearing turkeys which, again, proved unsuccessful. However, I remember some fun we had with the turkey eggs. Each day, the kids and I would search around the garden for eggs from the birds, but alas, no sign of anything. I found out the reason why our birds weren't producing eggs, or rather they were but not in our garden. The turkeys were laying their eggs in the garden of a hotel next door to our bed and breakfast.

We believed that the family who owned the hotel were deliberately keeping the eggs, without telling us they were from our turkeys. So Tony decided to take revenge. He crept into their garden late one night and replaced two of the eggs with rotten ones that I found a few weeks before. Next morning, we saw all the windows of the hotel being frantically opened to clear the rancid smell of the rotten eggs. We all laughed at that little escapade.

Morag and Stuart both loved the house in Kingussie. David Leslie quoted Morag in his book when he interviewed her about her life in the bed and breakfast house.

I loved those days when everybody seemed to be laughing all the time. The primary-school teacher lived just around the corner and was a wonderful lady who was so kind to me, teaching me to read and write before I even began school. She gave me my very first book to read and my very first word to write on my first day at school. It was "cat" – I remember it clearly.

I had so looked forward to that first day, meeting all my new friends, so proud in our uniforms with our hair neatly tied up.

<display ends>

Tony was making progress too. He was learning to come to terms with his disability and even thought about retraining. We found out that the local hairdresser was about to retire so Tony contacted the local employment agency and asked about funding. Because he was classed as disabled, he managed to get money from a government fund to learn how to cut hair.

We decided to move a little further north, to Aviemore. My mother lived there so it made sense for us to be nearer to her, so that she could help out with looking after the kids as they were growing up.

Morag used to watch her dad cut his customers' hair. Not to be outdone, Morag decided to try her hand at this newfound skill. Her best friend, Katrina, had lovely long curly hair. Well, she did at one time! Morag had made sure that Katrina's long curls looked a little "different". I was horrified when I saw poor Katrina. The girl's father was even more distraught.

We made a healthy profit on the house in Kingussie, so we could afford a nice home in Aviemore. It is funny though. My life had been spent catering for the bed and breakfast business, cleaning, tending to our customers and generally looking after the family. Now with both kids at school, Tony away training to be a hairdresser and no business to run, time was suddenly on my hands.

I first met Donnie Dempster while in Kingussie. He owned a local garage and he always watched the kids as they crossed the busy road on their way to school. Donnie and I started chatting, and our chats became more and more intense. I really admired him, mainly because he was the all-time self-made man. Donnie had started with nothing in life and had gone on to build a good business. Unlike Tony and I who had been given everything by Tony's father, Donnie knew what it was like to have nothing to start with. Challenge was the thing that Donnie lived for, and I hankered after something similar.

Tony and I used to meet up with Donnie and his wife. The four of us got on really well, but I guess I was drawn to Donnie. Whenever business took him to Aviemore, he would call up to see if I was in and pop round for a coffee and a chat. He was always asking after the kids, wondering how they were getting on at school.

But oh dear, our happy home turned quite sour. Tony listened to the local gossips who told him about Donnie's visits to our house while he was away at college. Our lovely new home in Aviemore was scarred with arguments, shouting at each other, and generally a very unpleasant time.

Stuart took the move to Aviemore really well. He seemed to settle into his new school quite quickly. Unlike Morag. She screamed the place down on her first day at her new school. She didn't know anyone so she was, understandably, very anxious about meeting new folk and making new friends. I think she missed her teacher at Kingussie. Morag was unhappy at school, and she was probably unhappy at home too. Tony and I would continue our shouting matches well into the small hours, often waking the kids, particularly Morag.

I continued to worry about the kids during that time in Aviemore. I wandered what impact Tony and I were having on them. That was no way to bring up youngsters, I thought.

Constantly arguing with each other, with little happiness, I couldn't take much more.

One day, I called my mother, and asked if I could bring Stuart and Morag round to stay. She agreed. So I packed up some things, told the kid to get some toys sorted out and we jumped into my car. I thought we could get away before Tony came home, but alas, it was not to be. He arrived home early as Morag was sitting in the car waiting for us to leave. It was quite emotional. I told Tony that we couldn't go on the way we had been living. I wanted him to visit his son and daughter very regularly, which I believe is the right way. However, I couldn't live with him anymore, it was just getting too much for us all. Looking back in the mirror, as we drove away from our house in Aviemore, I could see him wiping the tears away.

Life at my mother's was good fun. A little cramped, but we enjoyed our time there. Everything seemed to be working out, albeit, on a temporary basis.

One day, Morag declared "Dad is lonely. We are all together in this house, while my dad is all on his own." I did feel a little sad at that point. We never set out to wreck lives, but sometimes circumstances just happen. Morag was such a caring and compassionate person. She decided to move back with her father, while Stuart continued to live with me.

Years later, after my divorce from Tony came through, I became Mrs Dempster in the register-office in Fort William. We moved over to the east coast, to Forres, and built our house in 14 acres of land. When I saw that land come onto the property market, I knew immediately that it was the perfect place for us. Out of town, just a little, with loads of space for my horses, and a beautiful plot for the house, it all seemed exactly what we needed.

Donnie and Morag got on quite well together. Morag would visit us every week and Donnie took the opportunity to spoil her rotten. They would go swimming together and they would play in the garden. When she was 13, Morag moved back with us, in Forres. Tony, meanwhile, had met someone else, within six months of me moving out, married her, and they moved down to Tyneside. Sue was her name.

Morag suffered a little disappointment when she went to Forres Academy. During her first week, she was approached by a lad who told her that there was a boy at the school who shared her name "Dodds". "His name is Stuart Dodds, do you know him?" the boy asked. Morag found out that Stuart had never told anyone he had a sister. Maybe he was too embarrassed to tell people that his sister didn't live at home. Many years later, while Morag ran with her daughter from the clutches of the Chapmans, Stuart, once again, would fail to acknowledge his sister.

I think Donnie Dempster was probably the first person I was truly in love with. I had plenty of opportunities with other men but I think the chemistry between Donnie and I was unbelievable. I remember talking to my doctor, even before I left Tony, and he said, "You know Flora, you are like a teenager in love." At the age of 26, although not a teenager, I think that doctor was correct. Tony was a good man, a good father, albeit a bit of a scoundrel. But Donnie was different; he was my first true love.

I think there was a bit of resentment of Donnie, as far as Stuart and Morag were concerned. I guess it is only natural for kids to feel resentment for the man who had taken their mother away from their real father. I could never blame them for being a little off with Donnie, but he made the effort with them and I think Morag, at least, responded to that. Stuart probably reminded Donnie of Tony so perhaps that is why Morag and he got on a little better. Donnie was an incredibly jealous and insecure person so, again, that is maybe why he never really connected with Stuart. There was always a reminder of Tony. Of course, Morag was a more forgiving person than Stuart, so she was able to accept him into our lives more than Stuart.

There were many reasons why it never worked out in the end between Donnie and me. One of those reasons was his insane jealousy and paranoia that I was seeing other men. I remember when we were building our house in Forres, I had to be careful how I talked to the builders. The lads were really friendly and I would bring them beer during the warm days of summer. I had to tell them not to mention to Donnie that I had brought them drinks. Not because he would have disapproved of the lads drinking while on site, but because he would have immediately thought that there was something going on between me and one of the builders. Crazy level of jealousy!

He was a violent man as well. One time when we were at Kingussie, for something really trivial, he smacked me across my mouth with such force that it knocked out a tooth. I thought at that moment, I shouldn't be with him, but I kept persevering, hoping that his behaviour would improve. Love really does do strange things. I was madly in love with him, which is why I stayed and tolerated his violent outbursts.

Donnie did admit to me that it was drink that was causing his problems. When we moved to Forres, he swore that he would not drink again and that life would be great for us. The local doctor in Forres told me that it would never work out, that Donnie was too much of an addict for him to give up the drink. The doctor said that he would revert back to his violent behaviour time and time again. However, I was, as usual, quite stubborn, and really believed that it would work out. His brother and sister had both died as alcoholics so he knew the risks. All of those things, I thought, together with our new environment in Forres, would solve all of his issues.

How wrong was I?

It was his unpredictability that killed our relationship and marriage. I never knew what mood he would be in. If he was going to resort to violent outbursts or whether he was going to see the day through as a normal individual. I got to the point where living with him just got too unbearable.

Of course, we were living in the house together, as man and wife, so getting rid of Donnie was not going to be easy. Another factor that came into it was that I had a good business which was run from the house. I was supplying ponies for Riding for the Disabled. Every week I would provide ponies for the riders. The ponies were kept on the land that was alongside our house, so that land and house were classed as a business.

When Donnie and I decided to part company, we had to sort out the legal issue of ownership of the house. 14 acres of land, and my business. A long legal argument got underway and the case went to court. The sheriff who made the final ruling made an unprecedented decision, the first of its kind in Scotland. He decreed that, since I was running a business and that it would be compromised if Donnie and I sold the house and land to reach a financial settlement, he decided that I could "buy out" Donnie's share.

It was an arduous battle to get my case won, but eventually the sheriff agreed in my favour. I vowed then that I would never go through a court case again, not for this piece of land. Little did I know that my own son, Stuart, would battle me for six or seven years to get his hands on the house and land.

So, two valuations later, Donnie and I agreed on a price for the house and for the land. All I had to do was raise the money to buy out Donnie Dempster.

PHOTOGRAPHS FROM FORRES TO CONVINCE A JURY

Randy Berry advised me to take some video footage of Forres and the surrounding area so that the jury in Texas could see where I lived and where Morag's and Jasmine's home would be. So Don Evans and I set off around the town, taking shots of everything we thought were interesting. We talked over the shots, adding an adlib sort of commentary.

We went up St Leonards Road where Don used to own a large guesthouse. We visited churches, parks and schools, everything that we thought might appeal to a Texas jury.

Randy was supposed to get the video transferred onto the US television format and he said that he would get it edited down to about ten minutes. We shot more than 10 minutes, in fact we ended up taking about 45 minutes worth of material. Horses featured prominently in the video. Although he did get it converted into the American format, he never got around to editing the film, so the jury had to endure a lengthy presentation about the town of Forres in Scotland.

Forres is such a picturesque town. Winner of numerous floral competitions over the last 20 years, the town is usually awash with bright colours and an abundance of street flowering baskets. The town has won the Britain in Bloom competition four times. Organised by the Royal Horticultural Society, Britain in Bloom is a tough competition for a town to win. Thanks to the Forres in

Bloom Association, who is responsible for ensuring that flowers abound throughout the small town, the streets of the once-famous market place are cheerful with vibrant colours.

Grant Park, which is only a few miles from my house, is central to the floral display in the town. It is such a pleasure to take visitors to the park. Gifted to the town by Sir Alexander Grant, the park has a great collection of flowering species as well as trees and a sunken garden.

Another place to take visitors, or simply to stroll through to clear the mind, are the trails around Cluny Hill, which lies adjacent to Grant Park. At the top of the hill is the Nelson Tower, a tribute to Nelson's victory at the Battle of Trafalgar. I am not quite sure why the townsfolk decided to erect a tower in Nelson's name. I could never understand the connection between this small town in the north-east of Scotland and Admiral Nelson! Maybe if I had paid a little more attention in school, instead of dreaming about horses, I would have been able to see it. I wondered if the jury in Texas would understand. Perhaps not!

Apparently, the Forres "town crier" made an announcement in 1806. He said "It is proposed to erect, by subscription, on the summit of Cluny Hill, near Forres, a tower of which a plan, furnished gratuitously by Mr Charles Stuart, architect at Darnaway, is herewith laid before the public." The local people also thought that the tower would act as a useful beacon just in case the enemy were to approach the southern shores of the Moray Firth and plan an attack upon the town.

Now in the custody of Moray Council, the Nelson Tower is open to the public during the summer months. The view from the top, which stands at a little over 300 feet above sea level, is quite stunning. On a clear day, it is possible to see over to the Black Isle, well beyond Inverness.

Although history wasn't really my thing at school, I do remember a very enthusiastic teacher at my school in Keith, which is about 30 miles east of Forres, telling us that an important Charter was bestowed upon the market town of Forres. King James IV, on 23 June 1496, granted a new Charter to replace many of the older ones that were lost during various battles. It read

<display begins>

... that the ancient charters have been destroyed in time of war, or by the violence of fire, and grants of new in free burgage with the lands formerly belonging to the community, particularly the lands called Griveship, Baile-Lands, Meikle Bog, with the King's Meadon, Lobranstoun with Crealties and Ramflat, and common pasturage in the forest of Drumondside and Tulloch, with power annually to elect a Provist, Bailies and other Magistrates and Officers necessary, and to constitute the Provost and Baillies Sherriff within the Burgh and its liberties, and discharge the Sheriff of the shire of Elgin and Forres, to exercise his office within the said burgh or its liberties, with power to have a Cross, a weekly market, and an annual fair to continue for eight days, with all and sundry other privileges and immunities of a free burgh ...

<display ends>

And so the market-town of Forres was born.

Similar to other small settlements around the north-east of Scotland, the townsfolk decided they needed protection from possible invasion by the Highlanders. In 1588, a protective "dyke" around the town was commissioned. The protective wall would include town gates, or "ports" as they are often referred to. Parts of the wall can still be found in various areas around Forres today.

A watch or clock was not usually a possession of the working people of a small town, so the town drummer would walk around the community, beating his drum at 5am every morning. A bell was fitted to the clock in the tollbooth so that everyone had access to the correct Forres time. Of course, local time may vary considerably from other "times" in other communities. It was quite probable that, in Elgin, a short distance away, the time could be several minutes, even hours, different.

In 1603, it was recorded that the close at what is now No 96 High Street was to be extended back to the lands knows as the Hainings, which were let on a three-year tack at that time. Hainings was originally a term used to describe a well-watered meadow, but later became specifically reserved as a title for the lands where the king's horses were grazed when he visited his burghs to collect revenues and judge serious criminal offences. These visits by the king became important dates in the town calendar.

The years from 1638 until 1650 were a time of trouble during which Charles 1 attempted to force Episcopacy on Scotland, and in 1642 there was Civil War in England. Covenanter garrisons were stationed in Aberdeen and Inverness, resulting in all areas in between those cities being in constant turmoil. Troops continually passed through Forres, and they often stopped off to water their horses and to feed the soldiers. Town funds became stretched because the garrisons paid for very little when they ate or stayed in Forres.

At that time, the Kirk Session and the town Magistrates ruled against crime. Maybe similar to the Wild West of Texas, Forres was quite a rough place to live during the 18th century. The records show that, on 6 April 1702, the Town Clerk was ordered to advertise at the public market, that "if any of them be found swearing or drunken within this Burgh, that for each oath and for each drunkenness they shall pay 2 shillings Scots toties quoties." Expulsion of vagabonds and those with no "way of livelihood" was started, in an attempt to clean up the town.

By the middle of the 18th century, the Burgh of Forres was slowly beginning to recover from the dire financial consequences of the 1745 Jacobite Rebellion. The town was continuing to lose influence in the affairs of Moray, and

Elgin had now become the major community in the area. A garrison of soldiers continued to be based in Forres through 1750, and the local ladies continued to enjoy their company, some of these women being described as "lewd women in the town". Little seemed to escape the attention of the kirk elders!

Stricter planning laws came to the town in 1750, when John Robertson, a merchant trader, built a house that created problems for his neighbours. The formal complaint read "whereby he carries the front of his house quite out of the venal, and even upon a part of the venal, whereby his house is lyable to do damage in case of rain and speats to his neighbours. It is an apparent eyesore and deformity to the town, and yet it is the duty of the town to preserve the policy, ornament and beauty of the town as well as the property of the Burgh."

Oh dear, even then there were planning disputes. Nothing much has changed!

Around the middle of the 17th century, there were about 60 merchants and shopkeepers. These merchants would have travelled to Inverness, Sutherland and Ross to trade their goods, even venturing as far north as Orkney. A few mills had been built in Forres but mechanisation was starting to have an impact on the economic viability of those industries. There was high taxation in the town, to finance the wars with France and America, and the decline in industry in the area meant that the economy was struggling. The streets were polluted, dirty and an unsavoury collection of vagabonds and other undesirables frequented the place. In 1814, a police force was formed, and officers had to deal with many violent individuals. Grave robbery was rife in Scotland in the early part of the 19th century, so the police recruited night-watchmen to keep guard of churchyards.

Forres started to grow in population, particularly with the introduction of new industries, mills and farming around the town. A new court house was commissioned in the town in 1837, and, in the same year, a new gas works was built. The latter ensured that street lighting could be vastly improved along the main streets. A new church was built in 1841, and a qualified district nurse was appointed to look after residents. Smallpox hit Forres in 1838, killing many citizens.

The behaviour of teenage boys was of particular concern two centuries ago. In 1835, it was reported that boys selling pies in the town, obviously a fast food of the day, were inclined to be disorderly. As the complaints increased the council brought in some tough regulations. The minutes recorded

<display begins>

Names and ages of boys employed to sell pies to be given to the council.

Boys must not go along the pavements or stand at the shop doors or windows.

Boys are not to importune people passing, nor shriek, nor scream, nor cluster together. They must behave properly and go singly along the street.

The boys must find security to the extent of £5 for their good behaviour.

<display ends>

Perhaps the local council should consider re-introducing the laws of 1835!

Gradual improvement in the roads continued into the 20th century. Horse-drawn vehicles of earlier times gave way to motor cars, lorries and buses. Today, tourist buses can either stop off at one of the numerous hotels in the town for their holidaymakers to grab a bite to eat, or they can travel around the Forres bypass, which was built a few years ago to relieve the small streets of the heavy traffic that pounds the A96 from Aberdeen to Inverness.

Forres is sandwiched mid-way between Elgin and Nairn, both towns of Scottish importance. Nestled in the world-famous whisky region of Scotland, Elgin lies on the

A96 almost halfway between Aberdeen and Inverness. On North College Street are the lovely ruins of Elgin Cathedral and at the very top of High Street is one of Scotland's oldest museums, the Elgin Museum. To the west of Forres is the very attractive seaside town of Nairn. It is billed as one of the driest and sunniest places in Britain, because of the Gulf Stream that catches this north-easterly part of the mainland. During the Victorian era, thousands of people flocked to the town that reputedly had special medicinal properties in the local seawater. Today, the harbour at Nairn houses many pleasure boats, while the caravan park nearby is one of the nicest in Britain. The Nairn Agricultural Show and the Highland Games are attractions that bring thousands of tourists to the area every year.

The whole of Moray is wonderful, not just Forres, Nairn and Elgin. There is an abundance of history and heritage in this part of Scotland. Burial mounds have been discovered in the Moray area that prove it was inhabited around 1500BC. The area was hugely important during the Pictish period, being the heartland and kingdom of one particular tribe of Pictish people. The Romans visited the area but left without establishing a permanent base, and the Vikings also visited the shores of the Moray Firth. However, this latter people preferred Shetland and Orkney and, although they may have ventured south to Moray, they never actually settled in the area.

Moray, the coastline, the towns of Elgin, Nairn and Forres really do provide a great place to live, learn and develop. Jasmine could grow up here, she could learn about history, explore great sites, and develop into a well-educated young woman. She could become anything she wanted.

Don Evans and I had such a wonderful time taking loads of footage of the old buildings, schools and parks that provide such a scenic backdrop to the town. When we were taking those video shots, we couldn't help but think Morag and Jasmine would be happy here in Forres. I imagined long summer strolls, hand in hand with little Jasmine as we wandered through the trees of Grant Park. No doubt, she would ask me loads of questions, just like any other child of her age. Her inquisitiveness would, I expect get the better of me. I could imagine her asking "Granny, why is there a big building on top of the hill? Who was Nelson? Why did he fight people? Why did he hurt people? Why do people have to fight?" It seemed such a strange thing to be doing, making a video of my home so that people more than 7,000 miles away could watch it. Would it make a difference? I really didn't know, but it was a small price to pay if it made even the tiniest bit of difference.

As we shot the material for the video, I couldn't help smiling a little when I came across one of the roadside signs. It says "Forres is twinned with Mount Dora". The town is located in Florida and was formed in 1874. The settlement grew quickly after the first orange-picking house was built in 1891, to process the millions of oranges that were picked from nearby fields. A box factory and a fertilizer plant were constructed later in the 19th century, and a cannery opened in 1903. Thomas Edison, Henry Ford and President Dwight D. Eisenhower all visited the orange factory. The town of Mount Dora is noted for its crafts, antique shops, historical buildings and beautiful scenery.

A world atlas will show that Mount Dora in Florida is about 6,000 miles from Forres, and it is less than 1,000 miles from Austin. As we shot the video material, I smiled, just a little. Maybe there was a hint of Forres nearby my two girls. Alone and fighting an enemy, they most certainly were. But I would be leaving soon to join them in their fight. Maybe, just maybe, the "Forres twinned with Mount Dora" was a little omen that all would be well. Perhaps the church-loving folk of deep-south Texas would see that Jasmine could grow up with churches in abundance in Moray. Perhaps they would see that Forres, with its tremendous scenery, culture, arts and weather were all perfect for bringing up a healthy child. Perhaps they might even see that someone somewhere had decided to twin Forres with a town in Florida, maybe because Scotland and the US weren't so different after all. As I prepared to travel west to Texas I clung to the hope that our little video, my testimony, and the jury would all work in our favour.

I so hoped and prayed that it would.

THE VERDICT

The call came.

Morag and I promptly made our way to the court.

I think my hands were probably shaking as we sat in the cab en-route to the court room. There were probably only three likely outcomes, or so I thought. Morag, Marcus or the Chapmans. I went through each scenario in my mind. Which would work best for Jasmine? Another thought struck me. Out of the three options I wondered which one was the most likely. Two of them involved Jasmine staying in the US, with either Marcus or Lawilda and Jimmy Ross. Only one of those options resulted in my granddaughter coming back to Scotland.

I thought back to the bizarre court case too.

I suddenly remembered a strange thing that had happened. The guardian *ad litem* had been called to give evidence, which was quite convincing really. She got really close to the Chapmans so she knew a lot about Jasmine and about Morag. The judge had decided to "try a little experiment" during the trial, suggesting that "we do something a little more appropriate". He asked each of the jury members to write their questions down on a piece of paper, which was then handed to the judge. The attorneys would then go up to the bench and the judge would read the questions out to the attorneys, who then decided which questions could be asked in the public court. Terry Weeks said after the trial finished that it was "like a free-fire zone".

I couldn't imagine a sheriff in Forres conducting free-fire question time.

The jury asked through these "experimental questions", a whole range of different things. Of course, not all of the jurors' questions were read out publicly. But those that were read out were "interesting".

"Do you feel bad cashing your Government cheque considering what kind of work you do?" was one of the questions asked by a jury member. I would have loved to know which juror had asked that question because I think I may have kissed them there and then in the court room. Well, perhaps not!

"Are you ashamed of yourself when you think of how many lives you've ruined?" Wow! Great question, I thought.

I think Terry was quite confident after hearing the questions being read out in court. However, there was still an awful lot of doubt that could be cast in the jurors' minds. The Chapmans had spent a lot of time with Jasmine during the months following Morag's return from San Diego. The guardian had portrayed a good picture of loving and caring grandparents, a picture of a happy little girl, and a picture of a family that could more than afford a good standard of living for Jasmine.

As the court building got nearer and nearer, my mind continued to work through the events of the last ten days. Terry had called one of Marcus' former American girlfriends, who Terry referred to as a "trashy little thing". She talked about Marcus being an angry and violent man. Terry was convinced, after getting her testimony in court that Marcus was well out of the equation as a candidate for custody. The jury would have taken one look at Marcus' latest attempt at finding a partner and immediately felt wholeheartedly for Morag. In contrast to his girlfriend, Morag appeared in court in pristine condition, well dressed, articulate and, although clearly stressed, she portrayed the image of a loving and dedicated mother.

Marcus himself had come over quite badly in court. In fact, at one point during his testimony, Marcus exclaimed to Terry Weeks "I know where you live." After that outburst from Marcus the judge ordered him to stay well away from the attorney's address. In fact, and only in America could this possibly happen, the judge gave Weeks the authority to shoot Marcus if he ever came near him in a violent and threatening manner.

Another plus in our favour was a report that was submitted to the court from a child-protection officer from North Tyneside Health Care in England. She had been asked to examine Jasmine before Morag and she left Britain. In the court in Texas her report said "I found the assessment to be very satisfactory and was pleased to note Morag and Jasmine seemed to have a busy life attending local groups for mothers and toddlers, which they clearly enjoyed and an activity which I am constantly recommending to parents of children at this age. I did not find any cause for concerns regarding Jasmine's overall development at this time."

Go, Tyneside Health Care.

As our cab reached the court room, Terry Weeks' final address to the jury kept ringing in my ears. Morag, sitting quietly beside me in the cab, gave little away but afterwards she told me that she too had been replaying Terry's final words in that court.

Judge Dietz had lambasted Terry several times during his closing speech but, unperturbed, Terry pressed home his points. Terry opened his argument with a statement that hushed the court room. He said that the case should have never come to trial in Texas, alluding to the fact that America should never have got involved. He also alluded to the fact that England had let Morag and Jasmine down by failing to hear the case in their own country. I think Terry Weeks was dumbfounded by the English judges. A British mother and a British daughter being sent for trial in the US.

Bizarre! I would have loved to put those English judges in front of Dietz for a few hours, especially with Terry Weeks cross-examining them.

"This little girl was healthy and doing all right until she was ordered by some court to come over here on the basis of a lying declaration that Morag had lived in this country for six months." Terry continued "From that time on, this woman has lived a life of turmoil and hell."

Strong words. But would they have an impact on the jury?

Terry Weeks had ploughed into the guardian *ad litem* as well. "Were the little girl's needs put first by taking her from her mother, by breaking the bond she shared with her mother, by putting her with Lawilda and Jimmy Ross?" Before the jury could draw breath, Weeks answered the question for them. "No," he said. "We were punishing the mother."

Terry went on to talk about Jasmine in England and how well she was doing. He talked about Morag being a loving mother, a caring mother and a mother that would go to extreme lengths to protect her child. He talked about me, the grandmother, and he talked about a happy home that could await Jasmine back in Scotland.

There was no doubt about it, Jasmine bonded better with Jimmy Ross than she did with Lawilda. So Terry went to work on that one too. "She wants this kid," he exclaimed. His final blow to the Chapmans came when he talked about their age. "They are kind of old people," he said. "They are too old, they are too busy and they have their own work. They have their own jobs. They are ready to retire. They are retired."

Terry pointed at Morag and said "This woman has done a good job. There is no danger for Jasmine to be in Scotland. She was a normal happy little kid until we started helping her. We are asking that you award custody to Morag."

I remember the jury watching my video of Forres, the one that Don Evans and I had filmed. I watched their faces as they concentrated on Grant Park, on the High Street, the churches and the schools.

As those final words of Terry Weeks replayed in my head, the cab reached the court room.

On 23 February 1995, a jury in Austin, Texas made a stunning decision. I actually wasn't sure if I heard correctly at that time. I was numb, sick with worry, and frankly too tired to take it all in. Months of turmoil in England, trips back and forth to pack up Morag's house, the stress and worry with Morag and Jasmine going on the run in the US and my daughter ending up in jail in San Diego and then Austin, just got too much for me. I listened carefully but I think it was my subconscious brain that took it in.

By ten votes to two, joint custody of Jasmine Jamee Dodds had been awarded to Morag Dodds AND Flora Dempster.

I just sobbed and sobbed into my hanky. I remember Terry turning around to look at me as he hugged Morag. I think I just stared blankly at him. I'm not sure what he must have thought of me, after he had given his all to win the case for us and here was I just looking like a zombie. Actually, that was exactly how I felt, just like a lifeless zombie. The stress of all those days, weeks and months just seemed to pour out of me. We had won. I just couldn't believe it.

The Chapmans had been so close to getting custody of Jasmine, I was convinced of that. Lawilda looked shocked. There were gasps in the court room when the verdict was read out. Gasps and lots of murmurs seemed to spread from one end of the room to the other. Judge Dietz calmed his court room down and said very little. But he did say "Our legal system has let you down." I think of all the things that happened in the US, those final words from the judge just summed it up nicely. Morag and Jasmine had been put through hell because the US thinks more about people with cash to spend on attorneys rather than looking at the basics, a mother who was never violent to her daughter, a mother who loved her child more than life itself, and a mother who went to great lengths to protect her child. Of course, it wasn't only the US legal system that had failed. What about our own system back home? Those words from the judge just demonstrated to me that we had won over the English court as well. I certainly hoped that they would get to hear about this.

Now that Morag had legal custody there was nothing stopping her going straight out and cuddling Jasmine. That is exactly what she did. Jasmine was brought to Terry Weeks' office by a court official. It is amazing but Lawilda never even said goodbye to the kid. Not a "granny will be over to Scotland to see you soon," nor a "goodbye little one, we have had such a fun time together." Nothing.

Lawilda and Jimmy Ross made no acknowledgement of Jasmine. Lawilda did, however, say something to me. Her parting words were "That child is doomed, doomed. You better look after that child, Flora." I felt like smacking her face right there and then.

We had a strange situation after the trial. Jake Harris brought his kids along to Terry's office so that Jasmine could have other children to play with. So there we were, having just heard a verdict that we had been praying for but daren't hope too much, and now there was a kids' party being thrown in the attorney's office. There was such a mess. The kids were eating chocolate and crisps and there was juice on the go too. I think the kids took it all really well, unlike the adults in the room. Of course, Terry was quite relaxed about everything, well, apart from the mess his lovely expensive and polished table was getting into. I could see he was not very happy about that. But Morag, me and Jake, were all simply numb. Morag hugged and chatted to Jasmine and we made pleasant conversation but I think we all wanted to sit down, relax with a drink, and go to sleep.

Next day, I said to Morag that we should get Jasmine checked over by a medical professional. Jasmine screamed as the doctor tried to undress her for the examination. Morag was quite upset but angry too. Her little child had clearly been traumatised by her ordeal and, Morag and I both thought, what on earth had the Chapmans done to her? However, the medical staff at the hospital gave Jasmine the all-clear. Probably some psychological trauma but in all probability Jasmine would recover from that with a little care and love. She would certainly have plenty of that.

As for Marcus and his parents, well they weren't too happy. Not surprisingly, they vented their anger to a local journalist. Marcus was quoted in a newspaper

<display begins>

It's all motherhood and apple pie. This country's got that shit all mixed up. Justice ain't justice in America. I gave up a $100,000 a year job in Syria to come back to Austin and try to make a family. I didn't do that because I didn't care. I cared about my daughter, and I cared about Morag then, too. This case isn't about Jasmine. It's about hurting me, and she has done it.

<display ends>

I couldn't believe that he would have the audacity to say such a thing to a journalist. Of course it wasn't about hurting him. Morag, and I, had one objective and that was to get Jasmine out of that sodding country so that she could be cared for by her own mother. Marcus' feelings didn't really figure in that objective.

Lawilda let her feelings be known in the same newspaper feature. She said

<display begins>

The decision is no good for that child. When you pull 12 people off the streets who are nothing but labourers, they don't know anything. They come in with biases. They had a momma, and maybe she was loving and kind. They made their decision before they even came in that court room. The case should never have been heard by a jury. It should have been a judge. The jury's decision was based on motherhood and apple pie. That's this nation. But what they don't realise is motherhood and apple pie ain't what it used to be.

<display ends>

Go Lawilda, go. We all knew you were an arse, now you have just proved it. Perhaps Lawilda should have remembered the words of her fellow-countryman, Abraham Lincoln. He said "It is better to remain silent and be thought a fool than to speak out and remove all doubt." Yep, she certainly proved the point!

I guess it was easy for me to be really smug at that point, but I wasn't. Smugness and the sense of victory didn't come into it at all. Jasmine was a human being, not a piece of meat to be won over. She wasn't some sort of trophy that was awarded to the winner of the competition. No, Jasmine was a human being, a person that would grow into a beautiful woman. She was family. Victory was definitely not something that we celebrated. We were just unbelievably pleased, that's all.

Morag is a remarkable girl. She said to me "I want to show the judge how truly grateful I am, so I want him to meet Jasmine." Okay, I thought. I guess it probably wouldn't be too easy to get an appointment with the man, but Morag was not to be put off. She said "We are going to the court room and we are going to show off my little girl to Judge Dietz."

So, without much thought about what we were doing, the three of us set off, once more, for the court. We went through security at lunchtime, knowing that the judge always stopped at a certain time of day. We marched up to his office, knocked on the door and, before I knew what was happening, Morag was presenting her daughter to the judge who, only days before, had prescribed over the case. The judge handed a plastic wand as a present to Jasmine.

Of course, there were still some issues to sort out before Morag could leave Texas. There was the little issue of the kidnapping charge and there were the visitation rights for Marcus to be agreed. But there was soon to be good news. The Texan legal machine had decided that, for whatever reason, they would not be continuing with the abduction case against Morag. She was free to leave the US whenever she chose.

I decided to fly back to Scotland. I knew that there was still more work to be done between Morag and her attorneys to sort out the alimony and visitation rights, but I knew that all of those things could be done without me being there. Morag seemed uncannily relaxed now that the ordeal was over, so I decided to pack up and go home. I knew that it wouldn't be too long before Morag and Jasmine would be calling me to arrange a pick-up from the airport in Scotland, so off I went.

I left Texas with niggles in my mind though. Something in my subconscious told me that the end wasn't quite in sight. I predicted that Marcus and the Chapmans would take their time reaching an agreement with Morag's attorney. In fact, my concerns were totally justified.

I had been home in Scotland for a few weeks when suddenly Morag and Jasmine appeared on my doorstep. No amount of readiness could have prepared me for what Morag said. She told me that Marcus had been dragging out the meetings between the various attorneys. Morag heard that Marcus had gone to a meeting with Terry Weeks and Judge Dietz. The judge had become really frustrated with Marcus and had told him to "empty his pockets". A bemused Marcus emptied a few dollar bills out of his pocket, to be told by the judge "You are going to see what our jail looks like." Marcus had been put into a prison cell for a few hours because he would not come clean about his finances; he and his mother jointly owned property.

When Morag heard about this, she immediately started to worry about the fall-out. Marcus would be furious, so too would his parents. She packed her bags, told Marcus Jasmine had a doctor's appointment, and she headed for the airport. Once again, she had run off. The difference this time was that she did have the law on her side. She was now the legal guardian of Jasmine.

Not surprisingly, the Chapmans were livid with Morag. They went to the judge and complained vociferously. However, he was having none of it. He finally made his decision about visitation and care arrangements. Although the Chapmans and Marcus did come out of it reasonably well, he decided that it was perfectly legal for Jasmine to settle in Scotland.

Marcus, Lawilda and Jimmy Ross had been granted the right to take Jasmine to any country in Europe for up to two weeks per year, providing that country was a signatory to the Hague Convention. The Chapmans were given the right to see Jasmine for up to six weeks during each summer, in America. They had been ordered by the judge to pay for flights for Jasmine and to pay for flights for Morag too, if she wanted to accompany her daughter to the US.

In terms of monetary support, Marcus had been ordered to pay Morag about $920 per month and he would have to secure this with a $22,000 deposit to the court authorities in Austin to ensure that a regular supply of money went Morag's way just in case anything happened to Marcus. He was also told to pay $7,000 towards the car that they jointly owned in the US. And he was told to cover the cheque that had bounced, $385. Finally, Judge Dietz ordered Marcus to attend an anger management course!

As it transpired, Marcus never paid a penny. Morag had to support herself, getting money from the UK Government welfare benefits system. Marcus paid nothing to her or to

Jasmine in maintenance. The $7,000 that Morag received went to Terry Weeks, to pay his professional fees for the court case. The $22,000 was never paid by Marcus. So much for the judge setting out financial terms. Morag got nothing.

With Jasmine almost three years of age, a decent thing for the Chapmans to do might have been to let bygones be. I think most people in Lawilda's shoes would have admitted defeat, saw the benefit of Morag taking Jasmine home and let them get on with their lives. No, not Lawilda. She now attacked the judge. She claimed that he had been unfair towards them and that the judge had favoured Morag. Such was her anger, and such was her deranged state of mind, that she actually paraded outside the court house with a placard that read "Judge Dietz violates father's Texas Constitutional Rights".

Terry Weeks countered the formal complaint lodged by the Chapmans against the judge. Terry wrote

<display begins>

All of these acts by Mrs Chapman are, of course, to an extent understandable, in that she is attempting to help her son. But in doing so, she is using the judicial process in an inappropriate way and is causing expense for her former daughter-in-law. The pleading, on its face, is frivolous, and Morag Dodds should be awarded her attorney's fees for attending the hearing, preparing this motion and for studying the motion filed by Mrs Chapman. Reasonable attorney's fees for the above necessary acts are $200 per hour at the moment.

<display ends>

The final word in that long and bitter chapter of our lives went to Lawilda. She was quoted in a local newspaper as saying

<display begins>

We are going to fight this custody case. We were surprised to discover Jasmine had been taken away. All we want is a relationship with Jasmine, but Morag does not want us to know her. I was delighted when my son brought Morag home and said she was pregnant, but Morag disliked me for some reason. I tried everything to get along with her. I bought her clothes, and I bought her furniture, but there is only so much you can do. She is a very unusual person.

<display ends>

In contrast to the stories in the US newspapers, Alastair Bisset wrote a happy story that appeared in the local newspaper. I had bought a present for Jasmine, a lovely pony called Pip. The headline read *Jasmine comes home to a Pip of a present*

<display begins>

Toddler Jasmine Dodds was full of smiles last night when she was given an early third-birthday present – a pony called Pip.

It was a surprise welcome home present from her granny, Flora Dempster, who owns horse-breeding stables on the outskirts of Forres.

Flora, and Jasmine's mother, former nursery nurse Morag Dodds, won joint custody of little Jasmine in a Texas court in February.

But the biggest surprise of all was played on Flora, for she had no idea Morag and Jasmine were back home in Scotland until they were driven home to Forres last night.

The earlier-than-expected return trip had been made possible by America's Continental Airlines, which agreed, after being approached by the *Press & Journal*, to revalidate their expired air tickets.

"We were only too happy to oblige after learning about the circumstances of this case," said a Continental spokesman.

There were tears of joy and emotion as the trio were re-united with hugs and kisses at Forres last night.

The last time they were together was at the end of February, before Flora flew back to Scotland after the bitter court trial in the Texas state capital of Austin.

"It's brilliant, just brilliant," said Flora "It's the moment we have all prayed for and waited for, my daughter and granddaughter are back in Scotland. This past year has been a nightmare for us all."

As she hugged her mother in the courtyard of the stables overlooking Findhorn Bay and the Moray Firth, Morag said: "I can't describe how great it is to be back home.

"Driving up the A9 through the rain and mist was one of the most beautiful sights I have ever seen."

But she admitted: "I have no plans for the future, except that I know that life is going to be difficult for Jasmine and me.

"I just want to relax and think about things. I would like to go back to college and become qualified for nursery management, I might even open my own nursery. That would be great.

"But my main concern is Jasmine. I just want her to be happy and to lead a normal life.

"Marcus and his parents are welcome to come to Scotland any time for access visits, but I will never allow Jasmine to go out there alone. I will always go with her."

<display ends>

At least Morag was home safe with me in Scotland. Unfortunately, the story didn't end there. Morag never did get to train in nursery management, nor did she get to open her own nursery.

KEEPING BUSY

Morag and Jasmine returning home was absolutely wonderful. The initial euphoria, excitement, joy and tears quickly subsided, leaving the harsh reality that, as usual, life goes on. Morag was desperately trying to find work and she was making plans for her future. I had to return to some sort of "normal" as well. I had my horses, of course, and I also had my driving school, that I was now running on a part-time basis.

I qualified as a driving instructor in 1974. At that time there was far less bureaucracy involved with learning to become an instructor than there is now. I had to go from Kingussie to Aberdeen for a week to learn how to drive as an instructor should and to learn how to teach pupils.

Woman instructors were few and far between at that time so it was unusual to say the least that a woman wanted to learn to become an instructor. However, I had a young family to support. Stuart was living with me and Morag was with her dad, but I still needed income, so teaching youngsters to drive seemed like a good way to earn a living. Also, it gave me an opportunity to escape from Donnie Dempster for a few hours at a time, away from his abuse and violence, which had escalated to frightening levels.

Although it was a little easier in those days to get your licence to teach, there were still quite stiff examinations to pass. I had to take the written exam three times before I managed to get a pass. Then there was the driving skills part of the course, which was a doddle for me. I had been quite a good driver and, although I probably had a few bad habits like everyone else, getting those habits corrected was an easy task. Give me something practical to do and I thrive at it. But give me an examination to pass and I dread it.

The final part of the driving instructor's course was to complete the instructional test. However, after passing the initial exam and then the driving skills part, a person could start working as an instructor, providing they were working under an ADI (Approved Driving Instructor). This was good because it gave me time to practise and earn some real money before I needed to sit the final part of the course, the instructional skill test.

Initially, I worked under an ADI in Forres, Fearless Fred was his nickname. Fearless Fred apparently had "wandering hands" when teaching female pupils. He was an entertaining chap though. Unfortunately, well fortunately for me, he had a heart attack and could not drive. So I took over all of his pupils. It was then that some of the female pupils told me about his rather affectionate teaching methods. One person told me she had to shout at him to wake him up, after he told her to drive until he called out "stop", simulating an emergency stop. He had fallen asleep.

After a few months working for the local driving school, and after passing my final instructional examination, I started my own driving school business. I worked about 60 hours per week, and on Saturdays and Sundays. It is hard work being an instructor, with long hours and very few days off.

One day, a few years after I worked with Fearless Fred, and during the time that Donnie and I were splitting up, Donnie invited me over to our croft. I parked the driving-school car a short distance away and walked up to the house. He snatched the keys from me, ran down to my car, and took off the distributor cap and plug leads. All of this so that I couldn't start the car and so that he could get me back. I had to walk two miles to the garage. Luckily, the garage owner set me up with a new car.

I worked from the Elgin Test Centre. There was one examiner who was hated by most of his candidates. He used to come through to the waiting area and drop his clipboard onto a table about four feet from where the pupil was sitting. This unnerved most pupils who were waiting for their test to start. This particular examiner ended up going into a clinic to get dried out, several times. Another examiner went to work on one of the islands, and he ended up hanging himself.

It is funny, but in all of the years doing instructing, I have only every had one person damage my car. That was when one of my pupils, a Chinese man, reversed into a lamppost while carrying out a three-point turn.

Morag and Stuart were both put through their tests in Elgin. Morag passed first time, but unfortunately Stuart failed first and then passed the second time. I think the reason why he failed the first time was because he got "faily Bailey" as the examiner, who everyone knew preferred girls to boys. I delayed Morag going through her test for quite some time. I wanted to make sure she was really ready for driving before I let her sit her test. When she went to college, I insisted that she kept up her driving lessons. Her instructor had said to her "Morag, I have never seen anyone with such good clutch-control." Morag omitted the fact that her mother was a driving instructor!

I left driving instructing for a few years, but returned during the early 1990s. The British School of Motoring was looking for instructors so I enquired about opportunities with them. I had to re-do all the Government examinations because I hadn't been teaching for a few years and my ADI licences had lapsed. I passed without any problems. One of the things they made you do was to "teach" one of their examiners, as though they were a pupil. I passed that as well, but it was not easy.

I had great fun with the BSM. The money wasn't good because the BSM take their franchise fee off every week and sometimes you weren't left with very much. However, it was quite secure work, with lots of pupils.

The BSM had a contract with the army, so I was given the job of teaching two army lads at a time, from Fort George, a short distance from Forres. One lad sat in the back of the car while the other one drove for a while. They were given a maximum of 20 hours tuition; that was all. The army had their own examiners, so I would do as much as I could with the lads over 20 hours before handing them over to the army examiners. Most of those lads would never have passed the regular Government test, but I guess the army have their own way of working.

BSM had a cut-off point with the army lads, particularly if they were hopeless and had no chance of passing their army test, even after 20 hours. So, BSM would drop the hopeless lads after 10 hours. I remember one lad, who clearly fell into the "hopeless" category! The other person who was training alongside "hopeless" was actually quite good. So, we put the good one through his test early and gave his extra hours to the "not so good" one. When the army examiner came back from testing "hopeless" he was as white as a sheet, exclaiming "Who put him on test?" Obviously failed, which meant he must have been really hopeless for even the army to fail him.

Some months later, another batch of hopefuls arrived from the army for driving tuition. Guess what? Amongst the new arrivals was Mr Hopeless, and he asked for me specifically to be his instructor. Eventually, with a total of 40 hours driving tuition, he passed his army test.

I often think that being a driving instructor is like being an agony aunt or some sort of councillor. You get close to pupils, and they often want to share their secrets and problems with you. I usually tried to not get involved but I found that women in particular find it difficult to concentrate on their driving lessons if they have trouble at home. Drugs were often a problem too. Many times I had to stop the car with the dual controls because I thought the person wasn't paying enough attention to the road. Many times, the pupil would admit to me that they had a drug problem.

I had to drive 50 miles to one lad who wanted to do a week-long intensive course. He worked in a bar so he was late in bed most nights. He would yawn and yawn through the morning session in the car. He failed his first test. He wanted to get some lessons before he sat his test a second time. However, he wasn't working at this point, so I thought he would be more awake and more attentive. Not so. He was still yawning and yawning every morning. He failed the second test as well. The driving examiner said that the lad would stop at roundabouts and wait until other drivers started tooting their horns at him. Loss of concentration and loss of time-awareness are both signs of drug abuse.

I gave up driving instruction around about 2011. The recession hit the business quite badly and income from the driving school dropped sharply. I do miss it though; even the agony aunt part of the job was interesting, and very informative!

So, that's how I spent most of my time during the years after Morag returned from Texas. Morag needed help too.

PRYING EYES AND A HEART LEFT IN TEXAS

With Morag home in Scotland after the custody battle in Texas, life should have been returning to some form of normality for us all. Morag needed to start thinking about her life now and she had said that she might go back offshore, to get some money together for her and Jasmine to start afresh. That was no problem because I was quite willing to look after the child when Morag was away.

Morag went along to the council to ask about being allocated a house. They told her "Your mother has a house and you are staying there," which was quite true but we were really cramped. I didn't have a big house at that time, so space was very limited. She eventually had to go and stay at a hotel for a while so that the council would class her as "homeless".

After about four weeks, she was allocated a one-bedroom flat in Forres. Not ideal, but at least she was on the council-housing system, so perhaps she might be able to get a better place quite soon.

I went off to visit Stuart in San Diego, and when I came back Morag told me her latest news. She had started going out with a neighbour, a guy who had been known for his violence towards his wife. There is a court order now, banning him from going within a 10-mile radius of his new wife. When she told me she was seeing him I immediately said to her "He's bad news, Morag". The guy owned a tea room and Morag often helped out in the shop and at his auction business. I can't remember his name now, I just remember him as "Morag's boyfriend".

Morag and Jasmine joined her new boyfriend on a holiday in Spain. But Morag wouldn't leave her daughter in the evening so she stayed indoors with Jasmine while the guy went out drinking and dancing. Morag had bought a lollipop for Jasmine and in the evening she remembered that her boyfriend had put the lollipop inside his jacket pocket. Morag went looking for the sweet, and, to her astonishment, she found traces of white powder inside his pocket and on the lollipop. It transpired that he was a regular cocaine user.

I was furious with Morag when she told me the story. Not only that, Morag had confided in one of her chums, but unfortunately her chum had decided to tell others and before long word had spread around Forres. People were finger-pointing at her.

People used to stop me in the street and say things like "I saw your daughter down by the river, on the phone, while Jasmine played. She wasn't watching her." Morag told me that people were staring at her all the time. Everywhere she went in the town people would be obviously chatting about her as she and Jasmine walked past. Although Morag was quite lively and extroverted, the strain from the gossips and the continual scrutiny was starting to take its toll. Even her school friends had stopped speaking to her.

I was concerned about her behaviour. One day we were in the field with the horses when I noticed Jasmine running around quite near to a stallion. I said to Morag that she had better'd watch out for the girl, just in case the horse got frightened or startled. "She'll be okay," said Morag, nonchalantly. I think it was probably at that point I realised how much the whole custody thing had taken out of her. Plus, the publicity continued. There was absolutely no rest for her. A feature appeared with the headline *Mother in custody fight flees US with daughter*

<display begins

The father of toddler Jasmine Dodds, back in Scotland with her mother after an acrimonious custody battle in Texas, pledged last night: "I'll see my daughter grow up come hell or high water."

Speaking from his home in Austin, Texas, Mr Marcus Chapman said: "I am entitled to see my daughter and I will see my daughter. My understanding is she should not have left Texas until all civil proceedings were completed and they are not."

Ms Dodds, 31, returned to Scotland with two-year-old Jasmine, having unexpectedly left Texas without telling Mr Chapman, her former boyfriend and the father of the child, that she was leaving.

His mother, Mrs Lawilda Chapman, the headmistress of an elementary school in Woodville, Texas, said: "We are going to fight this custody case. We were surprised to discover Jasmine had been taken away."

Mrs Chapman said they were extremely concerned about Jasmine's welfare and worried that she would be brought up with immoral values.

"All we want is a relationship with Jasmine but Morag does not want us to know her."

Mr Chapman said he had never intended for the custody battle to become so acrimonious. He said his lawyer had suggested initially that he ask Morag to meet the terms of the Texas Family Code, which he said were the minimum visiting rights a parent who did not end up with custody would be entitled to, but she had refused.

"My lawyer said, 'Offer her the terms of the Code and save yourself a whole bunch of money and a whole bunch of grief and you will get the minimum anyway', and that's what I did. But she refused.

"I have spent $60,000 in this two-year battle."

<display ends>

What a terrible feature that was. Most of it was nonsense, because Morag hadn't "refused" to enter into negotiations. She was forced into the legal battle because of the pressure from the Chapmans. Of course, when people read these dreadful newspaper articles they think the worst; they think there is only one side to the story, which is why Morag was continually under pressure after she returned home.

Morag's boyfriend really was an evil sod. He used to claim that he was going off to do a house clearance so that he could sell the stuff at auctions. However, he was actually going off with another woman.

The relationship with Morag, thankfully, didn't last too long, but long enough for him to beat her up.

I felt really sorry for Morag. All she wanted was a stable relationship, someone she could love and someone who could accept Jasmine into his life. I think that's why she had so many false starts with men after she came back to Scotland.

We kept in contact with Alastair Bisset, the journalist. Morag told me that she called Alastair's office and talked to one of the sports writers. Morag had said to him "I know who you are, you are the handsome guy who sits around the corner from Bisset." He immediately responded by asking her out. Morag agreed.

The sports writer came round to pick her up. I told him "Morag has been through a lot so, if you are serious about going out with her, good. But if not, leave her alone." He told me that he thought Morag was a special woman and he wanted to treat her well. Unfortunately, Alastair Bisset found out about his work college going out with Morag. Well, maybe it was fortunate for Morag that Bisset did find out. He told Morag that the guy was married. Another disaster for her!

Morag told me later that Bisset himself was trying his luck with her. He took her to Findhorn for afternoon tea and I got a call from her asking if it was okay for me to look after Jasmine because she wanted to go to Bisset's caravan for the night.

So she lurched from one problem to the next.

She missed Randy Berry, I am convinced of that. Had she and Randy managed to sort out their relationship I think life would have been quite different for Morag.

While she was still in Texas, waiting for the access terms and visitation rights to get sorted out, she had become really close to Randy. He would ask her to help out with paperwork for some cases he was working on. She felt comfortable and safe with him. He even thought about moving to Scotland, to start up a liaison business. Families across Europe would need an expert in US law when they were facing similar circumstances to Morag. So he thought this would be a great way to live with Morag and work at the same time.

Randy called every day. Morag loved to sit and chat to him about her return to Scotland and about Jasmine and about her plans. She didn't tell him, though, about her boyfriends. I think she secretly wished that Randy could just fly over to Scotland and take her into his arms.

I could see my daughter slipping further and further downhill. Maybe she had been using drugs, I don't know. There were plenty of people around her who could sell her illegal substances. She was drinking heavily too. Enough, I thought, Randy needs to be here.

I called Randy and told him that Morag had a new boyfriend but that he too was completely wrong for her. I told Randy that she had a habit of picking up complete wasters and that, if he really loved Morag, he would get a ticket to Scotland pretty damned quickly.

In the spring of 1997, Randy arrived in Forres. He was amazed at the beautiful view from my home and he thought Forres was such a gorgeous town.

Randy was clearly distressed when he arrived here. I think he was very emotional, leaving his wife and telling her "I'm going to see Morag," and then arriving here not knowing what to expect. Morag freaked out when she saw Randy. Her new boyfriend was in the house at the time and I thought the situation might end up with Randy being attacked by him. Morag and her lad left before trouble could start.

I sat with Randy in my house in Forres and thought, it's too late. He agreed with me and said "I've left it too late, haven't I? I can't believe she has picked someone like that." Poor chap, he broke down in tears, and I knew then that he would soon leave for Texas and never come back. I was right. If only he had come to Scotland sooner. If only he and Morag had made better plans when she was out there. There were way too many "if only's".

And then there was the incident with the seat belt. If only that hadn't happened, maybe the spiral to disaster could have been halted. I had received poison pen letters, which had also been sent to the court in Austin, from someone who was infatuated by Don Evans, who of course, I was now seeing. We managed to find out her identity and Morag, in a fit of rage, had gone to confront this woman, Pauline was her name. Morag had shouted at her "What are you hoping to gain from this? We went through enough without you sending us those letters." Hearing the commotion on the street, Pauline's next-door neighbour came out to see if she could help. Pauline told her neighbour to call the police.

When the police arrived, Morag was talking with Pauline. A policewoman walked her to her car and told her to "Just go, drive off." Morag had been drinking but the police officer seemed to turn a blind eye. When they got to the car, the policewoman found Jasmine in the back seat, without a car restraint. Had Morag simply driven off at that moment, nothing more would have come of it. I'm not sure if Morag was being stubborn or if she really wanted to stay and try to convince Pauline to stop sending letters, but she told the police officer that she was okay and wanted to stay around. Of course, after numerous suggestions from the police that she should be "on her way", their patience ran out. Morag was arrested, breathalysed and found to be over the legal limit.

Don Evans picked up Jasmine and, next day, he picked up Morag from the police station.

Morag was banned from driving for one year. However, if that wasn't bad enough, worse was to come. The police officer who arrested Morag found that Jasmine had been in the car without a seat restraint. It is a criminal offence in Britain for a youngster to be in a car without proper restraints, so the police sent a report to Moray Council Social Work Department alleging that she might "wilfully neglect or expose Jasmine in a manner likely to cause unnecessary suffering or injury to health."

Meanwhile, the Chapmans were ramping up their attempts to cause trouble for Morag. They sent airline tickets to Morag so that she could take Jasmine out to Texas for a visit. Morag promptly ripped them up. During an interview with David Leslie for his book, Morag said

<display begins>

There was no way I was going back to Texas after my experience there the previous year. I had

travelled there expecting it to be more or less a formality that I'd quickly be back with Jasmine, but

look what happened. Now I was again being promised that all I had to do was to turn up and after six

weeks we'd be on our way home. No way. I believed I was being lured into a trap, that they'd find

some excuse, including the business of the seat belt, to have me back in court with

them, complaining that I was not looking after Jasmine properly and as a result was breaking the

terms of the custody order. Next would be the retrial they wanted.

Things just seemed to go from bad to worse. Lawilda and Jimmy Ross visited Forres about a year after Morag and Jasmine came home. I think their trip to Scotland was a mission to gather as much dirt as they could. And they were partly successful too. Apparently, a person who remained anonymous had called the social work department and told them that Morag had been shouting at Jasmine, at the same time as she had been drinking excessively. I think this information was passed on to the Chapmans.

Jimmy Ross was spotted talking to a local down-and-out, who all of a sudden seemed to have a wodge of cash to spend. Morag was convinced that a car was hanging around her place in Forres. We found out that the occupant of the car had been a private detective but, when we approached him, he wouldn't say who had commissioned him. A lot of people had been writing to the social work department to tell them "stories" about seeing Morag and Jasmine out and about and that the child hadn't been looked after properly. We later found out that a lot of these people had been in contact with the Chapmans, spying on Morag and informing on her.

A bizarre thing happened as well. Morag told me that she kept meeting a stranger. He kept "bumping" into her at odd times and places. Eventually, he had started speaking to her and, why I don't know, had persuaded her to take part in a sauna event in the town. She told me that she had taken Jasmine and they had both stripped off in the sauna. Apparently, the "event" was all about baring one's soul, as well as baring one's body! The really surprising thing was, shortly after the event, this perfect stranger disappeared. But the information about Morag taking Jasmine to the event lingered, and no doubt was passed on to the Chapmans as well.

All of those things that happened were more than coincidences. I really believe that the Chapman camp were spying on her and gathering dirt, which they would use at a later date.

Morag couldn't cope with the stress of all of this. She went downhill rapidly. However, she still had Jasmine and that kept her going. But her drinking was becoming a problem.

I decided that Morag needed to get dried out. I called Tony, her father, and explained the situation. He immediately agreed to pay for a clinic. Don had a few contacts and he managed to get her into a place in Inverness. She spent a few weeks there getting treatment, and she had counselling sessions with experts. I thought, and hoped, she would be a different person after she came out.

FAILED BY THOSE WHO WERE SUPPOSED TO HELP

In a recent article in the online *Guardian* newspaper a journalist said "A career in social work is first and foremost about helping people with difficulties they face. Social workers do this by developing a working relationship with children, young people and their families. However, families are complicated, so a social worker must always work hard to maintain a balance between compassion and making the right decisions to protect children."

A Director of Children and Families' Services at one council was quoted in the feature as saying "Social work is about supporting families but we also have to challenge families. Social workers have to work with a family to make sure it's strong enough to meet its own needs, or to identify that a family isn't going to repair itself in sufficient time for a child to thrive and be safe in it."

I think those were great words spoken by the woman who was interviewed for the article in the *Guardian*. I think social workers play a really important role in the community. But only if they do their job properly, which is "supporting families" through difficult times and helping family members to cope with life's problems. Supporting and helping, not working against families is the important thing. When done properly, I think the work social workers do is invaluable.

It beggars belief then, that the social workers at Moray Council completely failed in their "supporting families" role. Morag was hung out to dry by her so-called social worker.

Over a period of a few years, there were numerous reports commissioned by the Moray Council Community Services Department on Morag and Jasmine and the care that Morag was extending towards her daughter. The case in Austin was well documented and the council in Moray knew all about the outcome. So, why oh why did the social workers in charge of the case never actually "investigate" the findings of those studies? Why did they not work with Morag so that a way forward could be found? She was a vulnerable woman, who had been through a traumatic and stressful time, so why did the social workers not see this and help her rather than constantly batter her with the things that she had done wrong. To this day, I blame Moray Council social workers for the demise of Morag after her return from Texas. My opinion, I know. Others will disagree, but I really feel she was let down badly.

A woman who had given up so much for her daughter, had fought to bring her back to Scotland, and who had even spent time in prison in the knowledge that it might ultimately help in the end, was given no help when she eventually did get home.

After the incident with the seat belt, social workers placed Jasmine under a Child Protection Order. Jasmine's name was placed onto the North East of Scotland Child Protection Register. Moray Council gave the reasons for this as

<display begins>

1. A belief that Ms Dodds has a serious and long-standing alcohol problem which was adversely affecting her ability to meet her daughter's basic care needs on a regular basis.

2. A belief that this difficulty has been a significant factor in a number of incidents when it is considered that Jasmine has been placed at risk or in danger.

3. A belief that Ms Dodds has, and will continue to have, great difficulty in placing her daughter's care needs before her own needs.

4. A belief that Ms Dodds has considerable difficulty in accepting responsibility for her own actions or for her daughter's care and that she will continue to project that responsibility onto others including her daughter.

5. A belief that Ms Dodds has failed to benefit from professional intervention in connection with her alcohol and child-care difficulties.

<display ends>

I believe many of the reasons for the Child Protection Order were on the hearsay of what Moray Council said were "anonymous letters to both Social Work Department and school" that told how Morag was drunk while in charge of the child's care. Letters also claimed that Morag had been seen kicking Jasmine. Morag vehemently denied this.

And so, the spiral continued for Morag. Left alone, without professional care and help from the Council, she had to battle a number of enemies. People in the street would point their fingers; the media reported every small snippet of information; the Chapmans continually looked for an opportunity to exert revenge, and the council failed to provide adequate support. All those enemies acted against a lonely, broken-hearted woman who had been through unimaginable stress.

The media vultures were certainly out again. The Scottish-based *Herald* reported

<display begins>

A Scotswoman who won a bitter transatlantic tug of love for her baby daughter was yesterday put on probation for neglecting the child. A court heard that Morag Dodds lay sleeping while the four-year-old child in her care went into the street to play.

When police and social workers arrived at the house, they found 33-year-old Dodds in her bed. A bottle of pills and an empty vodka bottle were found lying in the next room. Dodds, of Strathcona Road, Forres, was placed on probation for 18 months when she admitted a charge of wilfully neglecting her child.

Elgin Sheriff Court heard how, in March this year, a neighbour had become worried about the welfare of the child in Dodds' care, who cannot be identified for legal reasons. Police tried knocking at Dodds' door, but when there was no reply they walked in and found her lying in bed. Dodds thought the young girl was in another room watching television, but when police could find no trace of her in the house Dodds admitted she had no idea where the child was.

<display ends>

Meanwhile, across the other side of the Atlantic, word had spread. With the help from the council and Morag's appointed social workers, Marcus managed to convince the Court of Session in Edinburgh to award him an interim interdict, which barred Jasmine from being removed from Scotland. I guess Marcus wanted to make sure Morag did not leave the country with his daughter.

The final straw came when an "incident" occurred one evening. Morag had gone out with the journalist, Bisset. His wife was away so he had invited Morag out to dinner. Jasmine was left in the care of a respected and well-liked boyfriend.

Morag and Bisset had gone in past Don Evan's place in town. He had an antique shop and they had popped in on their way home. Don said that Morag looked like something out of the television programme, *Dallas*. She looked a million dollars. Her dress was lovely and her hair was made up nicely. Morag had made an effort and she looked well that evening.

When she returned home, she found the boyfriend in a terrible state, with torn clothes and a badly cut leg. More distressing for Morag was the fact that Jasmine had gone.

Although the story is a little hazy, apparently a neighbour called the police claiming that the boyfriend in charge of the child was drunk. The police came and took Jasmine away. The boyfriend raced after the police van, with Jasmine in the back, desperately trying to stop them from removing Morag's daughter. He fell onto the street and was actually run over by one of the wheels of the police van. There was a tyre mark on his leg.

The babysitter denied that he had gone out of the house that evening.

Morag and Alastair Bisset went to the police station, but the police wouldn't tell them where Jasmine had been taken.

Jasmine was put into foster care.

Morag was losing her child.

In all of this tragedy with Morag there is still one burning question that remains for me. Why didn't the police or the social workers call me that night? Why wasn't Jasmine placed in my care? A court in Austin, Texas had awarded "joint" custody, so I had every right to look after my granddaughter, rather than putting her with foster parents. The ironic thing about all of this is that I was less than a mile away from Jasmine that night. I could have picked her up from the police station in about ten minutes. But no one called. Moray Council had dismissed the decision made in the US, based on an international law between Britain and the US, to award me as joint custodian. It probably suited them better to remove Jasmine from us altogether so that the Chapmans could get her.

On the night of the incident with the babysitter, Don Evans called the "out-of-hours'" social worker. He told them that "Flora Dempster has joint custody of the child. Why are you taking the child into care when the grandmother has custody?" But the social worker on duty that night was firm. He took Jasmine away from her mother and put her into care.

I tried talking with Moray Council, to try to find out why I was not being given access to the child. All my calls were rejected. No one talked to me.

Morag wanted to get her allocated social worker changed because she did not think they were bonding well together. Her request was denied.

I tried to get them to hand Jasmine over to me. I thought that would have been the ideal solution. The social workers could visit me anytime they wanted, day or night, to check on the progress being made with Jasmine and to check her mental and physical health. I had a house that was large enough for us and I was more than willing to drive Jasmine the short distance into town for her to go to nursery and even school. Morag could take her time, get her life sorted out, get her addiction to alcohol fixed, all in the knowledge that her daughter was safe with me.

But no. That was rejected by Moray Council.

Moray Council refused to acknowledge that I had any form of custody over the child. It is remarkable to think that, in Scotland, perfect strangers in the form of foster carers are preferred over a grandmother who has known the child from birth. A grandmother who, at her own expense, flew out to Texas to stand beside her daughter as they fought the establishment over there to get both daughter and granddaughter back to where they belonged.

But no. That too was rejected by Moray Council.

Even Tony's intervention did little to convince the social workers that we had a loving and caring family structure around Morag. Tony protested to Moray Council, stating that it would be detrimental for Jasmine's future if she were to be sent to the US. A better option, in his opinion, was for Jasmine to stay in Scotland while Morag sorted out her health and her life.

Once again, a great idea rejected by Moray Council.

The foster carers were actually nice people. Morag and I went to visit them and Jasmine. All Jasmine kept saying was "Granny, the police ran over a man!" Then the little girl said "Granny, come and save me. You did it once before."

The poor kid.

Of course I could have saved her, and I could have probably saved Morag too. But I needed help from the council. I needed them to recognise that I did have some degree of legal custody, but they refused to accept the decision in the US. They just blanked me out.

Jasmine stayed with the temporary foster carers for two or three nights before being sent to other carers. The social worker interviewed Jasmine a few times. "Your mother drinks vodka?" "No," said little Jasmine. "She drinks cider. My mother is just sick." Even a child could recognise that Morag was sick and needed proper help. Shame the grown-ups didn't.

The foster parents lived outside Forres so I would pop in when I was on my way back from a driving lesson. I remember one time I visited the house. Jasmine was behind the kitchen door, crying. Jasmine told Morag later "Granny came to see me but they wouldn't let me see her." I dropped in with clothes for Jasmine, but again, they wouldn't let me see the child. I can only assume that the social workers had told the parents not to allow me to see my granddaughter.

One of the saddest things I have ever seen was at Christmas. Morag wanted to drop a present off for her daughter. The social worker said "It's not convenient to go out and see your daughter at Christmas." We weren't going to be put off by this so I phoned the couple and told them that we had someone who could hand in some presents. Morag hid in the back of the car. The driver managed to get Jasmine to come out of the house to get her presents, so Morag at least got a look of her daughter. This broke Morag's heart.

A re-assessment of Jasmine was carried out by Moray Council Social Work Division. In their report they mentioned that Jasmine was being well cared for by the couple appointed to look after her. They talked about "risk areas" in relation to Morag looking after her daughter. Those risk areas were all centred around alcohol, the home environment and about her lifestyle. They also listed risk areas in relation to Marcus Chapman. There was a long list of things mentioned in the report, 21 items in fact. One of those risk factors said "Mr Chapman self-employed plus several other ventures – how much of his time would he have left for Jasmine?" Another risk in relation to Marcus was "Court ordered to complete anger management course in 1995 due to reported behaviour with Ms Dodds." In the report, the social worker claimed "Mr Chapman believes that Ms Dodds' father Tony will be supportive of Jasmine's return to him." No way did Tony think that. In fact, quite the opposite.

So, the report from the social worker identified numerous "risks" associated with letting Marcus take Jasmine back. In fact, there were more risks cited against Marcus in that report than there were against Morag.

The report also mentioned me. It said "Own history of use of alcohol." I couldn't believe it when I read this. When was alcohol ever cited as a problem for me? Of course, like billions of other people around the world, and like most Scottish people, I admit to "use of alcohol", but I completely resented this appearing on a report written by some totally biased social worker. It was years later that I found this report. The social worker had absolutely no evidence to back up a claim that I had a problem with alcohol.

So, with the social workers well and truly on their side, the Chapmans launched an all-out attack. Marcus travelled to Scotland. They had loads of ammunition against Morag. Her life was not exactly as it ought to have been and she had a stack of "criminal" charges against her, albeit for really trivial things. Possession of cannabis, to the value of £1.50, was one of the charges against her. Of course, the

Chapmans had one major ally on their side, Morag's social worker. In January 1998, the Court of Session in Edinburgh agreed with the Chapmans, and agreed with Moray Council. Jasmine was to go to America.

Within two days of the hearing in Edinburgh, Marcus, a man who had failed to keep up his financial support obligations to Morag, a man who had never sent his child a Christmas card, a man who had put his daughter and partner through hell, and a man identified as having "risks", boarded a flight with his daughter.

The final statement of Lord Nimmo Smith, the judge who presided over the case in Edinburgh said

<display begins>

Going to America will be a big move for Jasmine and is bound to cause her some emotional stress, because she plainly loves her mother. However, she is a bright and resilient child. She has already been able to cope and care for her mother when her mother has been drunk. If she is resilient enough to cope with that, then she is resilient enough to cope with a move to Texas.

<display ends>

It was probably more expensive for Moray Council to work with Morag and Jasmine. It was probably less expensive for them to recommend Jasmine went to the US. Money certainly talks! With patience, care, and perseverance, I believe the social workers could have turned Morag around. She was a broken woman, but one thing was in her favour. She loved her child more than life itself. Wasn't that a good basis to try and help?

I, and many other people who were involved in this terrible case, couldn't believe that the social worker allocated to Morag, didn't allow Morag to say goodbye to her child. She didn't allow her to hug her child for the last time, to say "mummy loves you", to say goodbye. Nothing.

Quite disgusting treatment from the so-called "caring profession".

I would love to meet the social worker now and ask her one simple question. "Did you, without doubt, provide Morag and Jasmine with the right amount of professional care that you were paid to do?" I rather suspect I know the answer to that question!

A family torn apart, by the very people who were supposed to help.

TIRED AND HEARTBROKEN, BUT ALWAYS A MOTHER

After Jasmine went back to the US with her father, I continued trying to contact the social work department to find out if there was anything else that we could do. Maybe there was something in the reports that were written about Morag and Jasmine that might help with a further attempt to get Jasmine back.

I contacted the person who ran the department but I had no success. It is a little ironic because his wife called me a few months later and asked if I would take out their son on driving lessons. I don't think they realised at first who I was so I agreed to take the boy out driving. He was a scoundrel though. He was in a lot of trouble with the police and was well known for hanging around Nairn, causing trouble, and for hooliganism. The lad had been rude to one of the local bobbies, so the policemen grabbed him. However, the family reported the bobby and he was suspended. The poor chap, he had been in Ireland, in the army, and had survived the troubles there, yet some hooligan managed to get him suspended from his job. Life really isn't fair sometimes.

I believed that, if Morag sorted out her life, then perhaps she would get Jasmine back. But she never did. She went from relationship to relationship, always seeking the love that she yearned for. Maybe she was trying to find a replacement for her daughter, but she never quite found the right person. It was agony watching my daughter sinking deeper and deeper into a place that was going to be difficult to get back from.

Morag started having epileptic seizures. I think it was probably because she wasn't looking after herself and her drinking was becoming a serious concern too. With no child to look after and no real cause in her life, she was letting go of all the fight within her.

She had become a media fascination. Even now, with Jasmine away in the US, her story still interested people. The headline in the *Daily Mail* in March 1999 read *Fears as love-tug mother vanishes from hospital bed*. It read

<display begins>

Police launched a search yesterday for a distraught mother who disappeared from hospital after losing a transatlantic custody battle for her young daughter.

Doctors called the police when Morag Dodds left her hospital bed when she was believed to be suffering from a brain clot.

She had been depressed since her bid to win her daughter back from her former boyfriend's family in America had been thwarted last year.

Yesterday Grampian Police put out an urgent plea for the whereabouts of Miss Dodds, 35, from Forres, Moray, who has not been seen since Wednesday evening.

Her mother Flora Dempster, who runs a kennels near Forres in Moray, said she was "desperately worried" about her. She added: "God knows where she is. The police arrived last night and told me that doctors at Dr Gray's Hospital in Elgin were worried because she had a suspected blood clot in her head.

The police told me she had walked out of the hospital. I gave them the names and addresses of everyone I could think of that she knows."

Mrs Dempster pleaded for Morag to get in touch.

Morag eventually did arrive back home safely. She was confused and knew very little about her own disappearance.

Morag was under enormous stress and strain during the years after they took Jasmine away. People in the town were constantly talking about her; she was finding it difficult to avoid the attention of unsavoury males; she had serious health problems and she was still being contacted by journalists. I remember one story though, which I thought was lovely. Even although Morag was under constant pressure, she still managed to think of others. The *Daily Record* ran a feature about Paula Yates and Bob Geldof.

<display begins>

Morag Dodds fought back tears as she read how Paula Yates lost custody of her daughters to ex-husband Bob Geldof. Morag, too, has faced the anguish of handing over her child to a man she no longer loves.

Her most treasured possession is a faded photograph of herself and her daughter together. But the happy times they once shared now seem a million miles away. And her greatest fear is that, with every passing day, she is becoming a stranger to her daughter, Jasmine, now six.

Morag, 34, a former nursery nurse of Forres, Morayshire, has not been able to speak to her little girl for months, despite repeated attempts to make contact. Her estranged boyfriend, American Marcus Chapman, took Jasmine to live with him in Killeen, Texas, last January after a court ruled he should care for her until custody is settled. Still Morag refuses to give up and is planning to take her fight to the European Court of Human Rights.

No one could have blamed her if she had admitted defeat a long time ago. Her custody battle has taken her back and forth across the Atlantic, it has seen her thrown into a Texas jail for child abduction and brought her entire life under scrutiny. And she is no nearer bringing her daughter home. All the battle has brought her is a tarnished reputation and a bill for legal expenses.

Yet the advice Morag offers Paula Yates is, "Never give up. No matter what they say about you, you never stop being a mother."

<display ends>

Those very poignant words made a lot of people cry. The journalist was quite right. Morag always believed that she was Jasmine's true mother. Although she was tired and struggling with her health, she kept on trying to think of ways to enter into the arena once more for her daughter.

We wrote to our Member of Parliament to find out about the European Court of Human Rights. I strongly believe that Moray Council had breached Morag's and my human rights. By going against the ruling in Texas, I believe they committed an error. I realise that Scottish law does not recognise a grandmother as a legal custodian but an American court had. I wanted to follow through all options available so we turned to our MP.

After a few letters back and forth, it became clear that an approach on the grounds of Moray Council breaching our human rights was not going to work. I received a letter from our solicitors that read

<display begins>

We must advise you that we question the merits of an application to the European Court of Human Rights in this matter. It is clear from the paperwork that you provided us that when reports were prepared concerning the future of Jasmine, you were one of the people interviewed and therefore considered, when decisions were being made about her future. Whilst you were not therefore able to attend the latter hearings the European Court of Human Rights may consider that the social work department discharged any duties that they may have to you in terms of your human rights. Further it is clear that the social work services group will take the position that as the joint custody order was not recognised in Scotland then they were entitled to exclude you from the hearings on the basis that you were not a "relevant person" in terms of statute. In any event the ultimate decision regarding Jasmine's residency was made by the Scottish courts not the social work department.

<display ends>

Unfortunately, one more avenue seemed to be heading into a dead end for us.

Morag was slipping further and further into depression. She called me and said "I've taken tablets and hoped that I would not wake up the next morning, and then I did." All I could think about was oranges. I thought how Morag must have had a really strong constitution before her body recovered from a dose of sleeping tablets. While I was pregnant with her, I craved oranges. I ate bags and bags of them. So Morag probably grew up with a body that was really healthy. Perhaps those oranges helped.

What could I do to help? I was running out of ideas.

The social work department was supposed to set up a video link so that Morag could see Jasmine but I don't know if that actually materialised. That might have helped her, to see her daughter safe and well. I did try and find out how Jasmine was doing over in the US but I didn't get much information from the council in Forres.

I found out later that one of the social workers from Forres went out to Texas to see how Jasmine was getting on. Apparently, Jasmine was asked "Would you like to see your mummy again?" and, apparently, she had replied with an emphatic "No." I am not sure if it is possible to brainwash a child so young, but I am convinced something must have been said to Jasmine to prompt her to answer the way that she did.

With little information coming to us from either the council or from the Chapmans, I decided to do something.

So I went to America.

I had kept up with May Cherry, the lady we met when in Austin. May was great, a big help when we got out there. I contacted her and told her that I was on my way to Austin.

I managed to find out where Jasmine was going to school. So I went along, but unfortunately, I couldn't get in because it was a military base. Then I went to the church which I thought Jasmine frequented.

An elderly woman at the church told me that she knew Jasmine and that she looked after her while Marcus was at work. I left a card with my contact details. Marcus turned up at my hotel that evening.

He called me the next day and said "We are going bowling in the evening so I will pick you up from your hotel."

I had brought over some Moray hazelnuts and made bramble jelly because I knew Jasmine liked those. For the entire car journey from the hotel to the bowling all I could hear from the back seat was Jasmine cracking open the hazelnuts. She loved them. She remembered Pip, the pony, and she asked about my other horses.

We didn't play bowling because we couldn't get a lane so we messed about with the one-arm bandit machines. Jasmine had a wonderful time, laughing and giggling and jumping around.

The next day I went to Jasmine's church. The lady whom I had met a few days before brought Jasmine along to see me. I wanted to buy a present for Jasmine before I returned to Scotland so we went shopping together. Jasmine settled on a set of horses in a box. We had lunch at a pizza restaurant. A tear came to my eye when I watched how kind Jasmine was. A little girl in the restaurant was looking longingly at the slot machines, but it was clear that she didn't have any money to play with. Jasmine watched the girl for some time before going over to her and handing her some money to play with. Morag had always taught Jasmine to share and be kind to people. That message certainly got through.

It was a wonderful visit.

Morag had been out to Texas before me though. About two or three months after Marcus took Jasmine back, Morag had decided to make the trip out there.

Randy met Morag at Houston. He contacted the Chapmans to tell them that Morag had arrived. However, the reply he got was not as expected. They told him that Jasmine did not want to go through with the visit. One can speculate as to why, all of a sudden, Jasmine had changed her mind. Was it because of the pressure exerted on her by the Chapmans? Was it genuinely that Jasmine felt frightened or confused so she had said "no" to the visit? Who knows the real reason?

Once again, another avenue that might have aided Morag's return to some degree of wellbeing was ruined. She returned to Scotland, even more devastated and broken than before, if that was at all possible.

Morag needed help and protection. All those who could have helped had let her down.

She gave a stark and honest interview to David Leslie for his book. She said

<display begins>

I have been betrayed by these people [social work department] who ought to have protected us instead of destroying us. I was particularly upset because I bought her [Jasmine] new shoes every three months, and every night she got a story and a wee singsong and a cuddle. When they took her into care, they never asked about what she liked when she went to bed or what kind of clothes she liked, their sizes, her favourite colours.

After she was taken into care, I used to see her for an hour at a time. One afternoon, I was helping with her homework when I was told my time was up. I was preparing to go, but Jasmine insisted that I help her finish, which I did. It meant the visit overran by a few minutes, which was held against me. I was warned that if it happened again, my visits could be stopped.

This was around the time that I was in a relationship with a businessman who had children of his own. His kids liked Jasmine and one day spotted her in town with the foster mother. Naturally, they went across to see her, but the foster carer said, "You must not speak to Jasmine." They were upset and wondered if they'd done something wrong. It was as if they had committed some crime, because I then received a call from a social worker, who said, "Look, we don't want this guy's children trying to talk to Jasmine."

When Jasmine was at school, I would go and visit her. There was a fence around the playground, but I'd wave to her and she'd come over to see me. I'd kiss her through the bars and say, "Sweetheart, Mummy loves you." But one of the supervisors evidently saw me and reported the matter. The social-work people then got in touch to say that I must not do it again. I thought, "What are you going to do? Shoot me?" I pointed out that I hadn't been in the school grounds, but they threatened to call the police. All the other mums could go to see their children but not me. It was horrendous, especially because Jasmine was always proud to be with me.

I hope those who stopped this are proud of themselves. Maybe they have children. Well, no doubt they are pleased at ensuring I'm no longer with mine. Maybe there will come a day when they are no longer with their children. Then they'll know what I go through every minute of every day.

That kiss was the last one I was ever able to give my daughter. When a reporter came to tell me she had been taken to America, I kept asking him, "How could they have done that without telling me?" I didn't even get the chance to say goodbye to her. I didn't even get the chance to reassure her. Nothing. She was just taken away. She didn't know what was going on, and I didn't know what was going on.

Now, there isn't a day when I don't think about her, but I seem to have fallen into an abyss of despair. I drink a lot and have health problems, but they are all because of not having Jasmine.

I have tried overdosing three times but stop because I tell myself that if I go ahead I won't ever get to see her again. Then I look in the mirror to see just how much I seem to have aged and say "I don't want you to see me like this, Jasmine. This isn't the mummy you knew. Maybe you wouldn't even recognise me."

I know many people will say that the condition I am now in is my fault. Well, maybe part of it is, but when Jasmine and I were together things were fine. It was only when Marcus came on the scene and started throwing money around to take Jasmine away that my life began going wrong. All I ever wanted was to be with children and now the only child I have I can't see.

<display ends>

Morag sent presents to Jasmine. For her tenth birthday, she sent a St Christopher necklace and a cake. Although we never knew whether Jasmine received the presents, we did get a message the same year that Jasmine was ten. Morag got a letter from Jasmine, which read

<display begins>

Sorry I have not written to you before now but I have been so busy with school and gymnastics, sports and church.

Besides church on Sunday, I work with four-year-olds on Saturday mornings.

I am really getting good at diving and swimming since I practice every day.

I am sending you this bible for you to read and learn the right way to change your life.

I hope you really read it.

Love Jasmine.

<display ends>

I could be wrong, but I think perhaps other people had a hand in writing those words.

I am not sure if the letter and bible from Jasmine really helped Morag. I guess there was a sparkle in her eye when she read the letter. But I think she was too depressed to really understand what was going on. Her medication was quite strong, so it all had the effect of confusing her. The *Evening Express* ran a short feature

<display begins>

A mum who lost custody of her daughter in a transatlantic tug of love has gone missing. Morag Dodds. 42, disappeared from her Fraserburgh home on Boxing Day after spending Christmas Day with her mum Flora Dempster. Mrs Demspter of Forres said Morag was still devastated by the loss of her child.

<display ends>

Morag did eventually turn up. She had gone off to stay with friends. Christmas Day left all sorts of strange memories for her. She kept thinking back to that time in the British Consulate-General office, where she managed to get some money to pay for a cab and hotel for the night. Christmas to Morag is associated with trauma, being in jail and the start of the journey without Jasmine. It was little wonder that she took off to live with her chums for a while. If only she had told me that was what she was planning.

Months later, and out of the blue, I received a call from her one day. She said "I've been to hospital." Morag, without telling me, had been diagnosed with cancer of the tongue. She had been to get an operation, which involved taking a chunk of muscle from her leg and rebuilding her tongue. She had gone to her dentist for a check-up and he had sent her to hospital, where they found cancer in her mouth. Her tongue had to be cut out and all the cancer removed. An 11-hour operation to rebuild her mouth had to take place. She could speak but she had a definite lisp. I knew nothing about it because Morag didn't want to worry me.

Morag couldn't eat properly so she was on high-protein milk drinks. She really looked awful when I saw her. A skeleton of her former self. She had psoriasis all over her body. She was seeing Jack Reeves in Fraserburgh and I think she was being supplied with all sorts of drink and drugs. Her body was slowly shutting down. I went to see her one day and we went to a little tea room near to Banff. She had Cullen skink. She loved that and she could eat it quite easily. There were three boys speaking to the guy who owned the tea room. They were swearing quite a lot. Morag said to them "Don't talk like that in front of women. That's not the done thing to do." I wondered if the boys would take a swing at her, but they didn't. Even at the very last, she was always keen that people did the right thing.

That was the last time I saw my daughter.

Morag died on 22 December 2008.

At least she didn't have to endure another Christmas Day.

DREAMS ARE HARD TO FOLLOW

Mariah Carey wrote the song *Hero* originally for the Dustin Hoffman movie by the same name. However, the producers of the movie preferred another song but Carey was convinced by her producer to record *Hero* for her latest album. Regarded as one of her most inspirational hits, the song's protagonist declares that, even though we may feel discouraged or down at times, in reality we are all "heroes" if we look inside ourselves and see our own inner strength.

Morag certainly had more than enough inner strength. I think it is testimony to her upbringing and possibly to the genes of our forebears. Our clan was known for its resolve and for their appetite for living life. Morag will be known for those things too, but she will also be known for her courage and for her love. She loved her daughter and she was hugely courageous, even to the extent of going to prison. She gave everything to fight those who wanted to stop her being with her daughter. She even gave her life.

The chorus of *Hero* is, simply, Morag.

<display begins>

And then a hero comes along
With the strength to carry on
And you cast your fears aside
And you know you can survive
So when you feel like hope is gone
Look inside you and be strong
And you'll finally see the truth
That a hero lies in you

Sure, there will be people who will condemn her for her actions. Why didn't she make it up with the Chapmans, find a compromise? Why didn't she look after her health so that she could care for Jasmine? Why didn't she work things out with Marcus, and why did she take up with so many undesirable men? Maybe she was hoping that her own hero would come along and give her the two things she most wanted out of life, her daughter and the love of a decent man. She got neither in the end.

But Morag was a true hero to Jasmine. She fought until the last breath in her body was gone. She did more than many, in fact more than most. Most people would have thrown in the towel long before she did. But she was up against a stack of people. The Chapmans, who so wanted the little girl, the court in England, the social workers, and the guys she hung out with. If only.

I couldn't face dealing with all the things associated with arranging a funeral, so I asked Tony, Morag's father, to take over. I just couldn't cope with emptying her house and dealing with all the stuff that needed to be done. I think I was like Morag, tired.

Tony arranged the cremation, which took place 80 miles from Forres. He hadn't thought about a church service so I had to arrange that. I talked to the local minister and told him about Morag. I picked out some hymns and other music and arranged an after-service tea. Tony paid for the funeral but he refused to pay for the tea because he said he wouldn't be attending it.

Tony contacted his stepson, Fraser. He lived in Nethy Bridge, which was quite near. I found out later that Tony had called the council and arranged for them to go in and clear everything from Morag's house. All her photographs and personal treasures, which should have gone to Jasmine, were dumped.

Morag was found in her bed. A combination of alcohol and the cancer killed her. Her body was so weak that I don't suppose it took much alcohol to tip her over the edge. She probably only had a glass or two of wine, on top of all the drugs that she was on for the pain and for her mouth.

The funeral was on Tuesday 13 January 2009.

Rachael, Stuart's daughter, who was an accomplished singer, had asked if she could pay a tribute to Morag. She sang *Hero*. It was beautiful. It was poignant. It was truly lovely.

Neither Stuart nor Marcus attended the funeral.

But a lot of people did attend St Laurence Church in Forres. Built in 1904, the site of the present church has been a place of worship since the middle of the 13th century, when Alexander III erected a chapel in honour of St Laurence as a memorial to his late wife Margaret. The main spire reaches a height of 120 feet and inside there is a wonderful marble baptismal font. The building is simple but lovely, and so too was the exquisite melody from Rachael reverberating around the walls and into the hearts of those who attended. Many people commented afterwards what a beautiful thing it was for Rachael to have done.

<display begins>

Lord knows

Dreams are hard to follow

But don't let anyone

Tear them away

Hold on

There will be tomorrow

In time you'll find the way

<display ends>

The service was conducted by Reverend Barry Boyd, and included the hymn *All Things Bright and Beautiful* and the song *Morning has Broken*. I asked for the Frankie Miller song, *Darlin*, to be played as the coffin was carried from the church. I thought it would be a nice message, from Morag to Jasmine.

<display begins>

Darlin'
Love you more than ever
Wish we were together
Darlin' of mine.
Darlin'
I'm feeling pretty lonesome.
<display ends>

Morag's final resting place is under the bridge of the River Spey at Kingussie. I planted some flowers and put up a little sign on a tree.

<extra line space>

I worked on creating a Family Tree, which I sent to Jasmine in 2010. I wrote a little note to go with it.

<display begins>

Enclosed for your birthday is a Family Tree, which I hope you will keep safe. Your mum was really into "being a Scottish lady" and she would have liked you to follow in her footsteps.

I am sure you will.

I have also enclosed the last things the police gave me from your mum – her purse, its contents and her rings.

<display ends>

Four years on, I am still waiting for a reply from Jasmine.

I found out from Tony, Morag's father, that Jasmine had been in the UK, the year before Morag died. Lawilda had brought her over to Newcastle but hadn't told me that they were in the country. I asked Tony why he had entertained Lawilda at his home after all the hurt she had caused our family. Tony never really answered my question. On Facebook, Jasmine was asked by Rachael, Stuart's daughter, why she hadn't visited Scotland. Jasmine replied that she had asked Lawilda if they could visit her mother but Lawilda had said an emphatic no. She had added "When you are 18 years old, you can do what you want."

Morag died a year after Jasmine's visit to Newcastle. It would have greatly upset Morag to know that Jasmine was in the UK and had not come up to Scotland to see her. Of course, it wasn't Jasmine's fault, it was Lawilda who had prevented her from seeing her mother. I can only hope that Lawilda sees how tragic that decision was.

How had such a beautiful girl ended up dying at such an early age? Such a waste of talent and such a waste of the love that she could have given to others. Morag loved children, which is why she studied nursery care.

Of course, this tragedy is not down to one person. Some of the blame lies with Morag, but some also lies with others. Human beings are all too often so caught up in their own lives, in their own dreams and in their own selfish needs that they ignore the needs of others. I am critical of the Chapmans, I think that is obvious. But I do believe they played their part in Morag's downfall. She was their daughter-in-law so why not treat her with respect? They wanted to win, regardless.

I am also very critical of the social workers. But I'm not the only one. Don Evans too was disapproving of the contribution they had made, particularly with regard to supporting Morag. He says "There was no involvement of social work prior to the court case. It was only upon the return of the child to Scotland that social workers became involved. But when Morag came back, she was, of course, as high as a kite with all the local and international publicity, and she coped poorly with that. At that time, I felt that there should have been support given to both mother and child."

Morag coped really badly with the aftermath of the court case and with the publicity. I guess it is difficult to know how any of us will react when we are placed under such strain. Like all materials, we have a breaking point. Some of us break easily and need help early. Some of us can press on for months and years, absorbing the strain, before we finally cave in and break. But I believe we all break at some point.

How did I manage to get through the years following the death of my daughter? I guess I just had to.

The battle with Stuart took up some of my time.

Also, I bought a nice penthouse in the Turkish part of Cyprus, where I can escape to every so often. I feel really at home there because there are lots of Scots. In fact, some of the people near to my place in Cyprus live within 11 miles of my house in Forres. I have really helpful neighbours who buy milk and eggs for my arrival.

I go out to Cyprus about twice a year. Life is very laid-back there.

I keep a little car out there, so that I can travel around the area. The MOTs are funny in Cyprus. Although they have to be carried out every three years, just like the UK, the tests are quite different to those in this country. A quick engine-number check and, bizarrely, a check to see if there are mud flaps and that is about it. No road test, brake tests or other safety checks, just mud flaps!

There is a horse-racing course just across the border, into south Cyprus. I went there with two neighbours one afternoon. We just walked in without any checks being carried out. An Irish horse won a race so my neighbour, being Irish, went into the winning enclosure and handed over her camera to one of the official photographers. He then took a photograph of her posing beside the winning horse. Can you imagine trying that at Ascot? Britain used to be like Cyprus until bureaucracy went mad.

As far as Don Evans is concerned, I ended our relationship. I got fed up with the women whom he met through his work causing trouble. One person sent a Valentine's card to my address, even although Don and I were actually living above his antique shop, saying that she was looking forward to his next visit. A parcel arrived, addressed to me. It had one sock inside. The sender said that the sock had been left behind and she went on to say that Don was "not half the man he used to be", exclaiming that "perhaps he is spreading himself too far."

In an evening, the phone would ring but when I answered the caller would hang up. When it rang a second time, Don would take the phone into his shop to speak. Another time, a message was left on the answer machine, whereby the woman simply said "I guess I know the answer now."

A steady stream of women used to turn up. On one occasion he asked me to leave so that he could talk to the woman, apparently about her marriage breakdown.

I think there were lots of similarities between Don and Marcus. Don's father would go off "out on the town" on many occasions. Don's mother devoted herself to her two sons, in particular Don. In later years, she would call him three or four times a day, just like Lawilda used to do with Marcus. She would shop for clothes for him and she would stay with him and his former wife every weekend. Whenever Don moved house, his mother would buy one nearby.

I am still friends with Don. Don and I have shared our troubled times together and he has been very supportive. He is now married to a Chinese lady, whom he found through a website. He went off to China and was asked to choose one of the women on parade there. I think the culture in China suits Don; men do as they like and the wives take a backseat.

His mother died recently, at the age of 101.

So life at the moment continues alone. Now Morag has gone, I dread Christmas and the New Year. I never put up a Christmas tree or decorations. I could go away on holiday during the festive period but when I see other people celebrating it just makes me sad. I usually spend the occasion at home, wishing time away, and looking forward to spring.

At least Morag's pain is no longer a problem. Her heart had been broken. I remember her telling me that her doctor had said to her "Morag, I don't have a pill for a broken heart." Although I have very sad memories of her, I also have happy memories too.

I have just been looking after one of Morag's school friend's dogs. She told me "What a gorgeous person Morag was," going on to add "We all loved her at school." Morag certainly had a keen sense of humour. Her friend told me that one day she remembered Morag leaving the house on a pushbike, with Jasmine behind her. However, with a lot of twists and turns on the track from the house down to the main road, Morag gave up. She abandoned her bike and walked. On her return, her bike had been stolen so she called the police to report it missing. The policeman who took the call asked her where the bike was last seen. Her reply was "left from the croft, third bush on the left, that's where I fell off last."

I am convinced that, one day, Jasmine will read my words. She will perhaps see something on the internet about this book, or she might simply have a need to find out more about her mum. I am convinced too that, when that day comes, when she reads about her mum's passionate and relentless fight to keep her daughter until the day that life left her body, Jasmine will realise, her mum was a true hero.

<display begins>
So when you feel like hope is gone
Look inside you and be strong
And you'll finally see the truth
That a hero lies in you.
<display ends>

OUR FAMILY TREE

Following Morag's death in 2008, I absorbed myself in researching our past. Family history is a wonderful hobby and it is amazing what can be found out with a little patience and dogged determination.

I managed to get back to about 1752, when William Macdonald married Elspeth Grant in Inveravon. They had a son, Patrick, who married Helen Dean. One of their children, Robert Macdonald, was my great-great-grandfather.

The parish of Inveravon is about 11 miles from Grantown. Deriving its name from its location at the mouth of the river Avon, it lies at the foot of the spectacular mountain of Ben Macdui and the Cairngorms. In 1594, a very famous battle occurred in this parish, whereby the Earl of Huntly defeated the Marquis of Argyle. The population in 1755 was 2,464.

Another very noteworthy event happened a little more than a century after that first battle, and involved the Grants, possibly the forbears of the Grant family in my lineage.

James Grant was a troublesome individual. In the reign of Charles I, James Grant is referred to in historical records as James an Tuim. He is mentioned as one of the ringleaders in the "treacherous abduction of the young laird of Ballindalloch". Grant spent some time in prison in Edinburgh Castle but managed to escape using ropes to scale down the walls. He returned to Speyside and met with some acquaintances. However, more dastardly deeds were to follow, because he murdered a father and two sons, slicing their heads off and sending them to the wife and mother.

Robert Macdonald married Margaret Garron in 1822. They had ten children, one of whom was William Macdonald, christened in 1824. He went on to run the 964-acre Tomnarieve Farm, in the parish of Inveravon. He married Helen Beattie in 1865 in the Cabrach, the name of which means "antler place" in Gaelic.

William and Helen had six children, including my grandfather, William Alexander Macdonald. Born in 1872, my grandfather lived until a heart attack killed him at the age of 60. His sister, Mary Ann, died just a few days before him. Mary Ann and her husband, Patrick Grant, owned the Delnasaugh Hotel in Glenlivet. William married Elizabeth Murray in Keith in 1907.

In Glenlivet about three-fifths of the people are Roman Catholics. There are two Roman Catholic chapels, one at Tombia, pretty far up the glen, the other at Chapelton, in the Braes of Glenlivet. The parish church was built in 1806. It was intended for the accommodation of the Protestants in Glenlivet, as well as the ordinary congregation, and seated about 550 people. There was no chapel of ease in the parish but there was a mission supported by the Royal Bounty that had been in operation in Glenlivet for upwards of 100 years.

My mother, Flora Macdonald, was one of nine children. She had a twin, William, who was killed in action in Italy in 1944 while serving with the Seaforth Highlanders. My mother married Charles James Simpson, a grocer, in Elgin in 1937. They had two children, Norman, who was born in 1938, and, five years later, me.

And finally, at the bottom of our family tree is Jasmine and her two cousins, Rachael, born to Tracy Carrington, and Natalie born to Dena Carpenter. Rachael and Natalie are Stuart's daughters.

Still a work-in-progress, the family tree will continue to be worked on. However, as it stands, it is a great souvenir. I hope Jasmine will, one day, take over from me to keep our family tree up to date.

EPILOGUE

The reason I embarked upon writing this book and creating a family tree was for Jasmine. I am convinced the day will come when Jasmine will look back at her life and start asking questions about her mother and her grandmother. So this book, and the family tree, are for Jasmine, and for her children.

I believe the injustices that occurred in England, in Texas and in Scotland had far-reaching effects, damaging a family beyond repair. No one is perfect, certainly not me nor my daughter, Morag. We all played our part in this sad story. We all got things wrong. But, I believe one group of people more than any other had a key role to play, and they failed miserably. I am not talking about the courts, and I am not even talking about the Chapmans. I am talking about the decisions made by the so-called "professional" people.

Judge John Deitz said that he had never in his career disagreed with a jury. So why did Moray Council? I had joint custody of Jasmine, yet they rejected this wholeheartedly, saying that the verdict did not apply in Scotland. The council social workers took Marcus' side and produced a compelling case to the court in Edinburgh to let Marcus take Jasmine away from her mother, and from me. A man, whom the American court had declared as unsuitable to care for Jasmine, was awarded custody by a Scottish court, aided by the social workers of Moray Council. Quite unbelievable. Quite tragic. Quite irresponsible, in my view.

I believe it was a travesty that this happened. Sure, I do not think for one minute that Morag was blameless. She had a few problems and those problems needed sorting out. Support was the one thing she needed, and support was the one thing she did not get. To this day, I believe that Jasmine would have grown up a Scottish lass in our beautiful country had those professionals taken a good hard look at Morag and helped her to achieve her one aim in life, to be a loving mother. Morag had the fundamentals already in place. She was a loving mother. Her heart was truly in the correct place. She loved Jasmine more than life itself. But, she just couldn't cope with the pressure and stresses that the Chapmans had bestowed upon her. She could have coped though. Had she been given a decent and caring social worker to partner with her, to guide and support her through the tough times and to be there when she most needed that support, Morag could have made it.

There were many sad aspects to this story. One of the most tear-wrenching of them all was Jasmine's first day at school. Morag had saved up really hard to buy Jasmine her first school uniform. She was more excited about that first day than Jasmine was. However, the social workers refused to allow Jasmine to wear her new uniform because it had been bought by Morag. Instead, they encouraged Marcus to "sponsor" Jasmine's first day at school and donate some money for her new clothes. As the other proud mothers stood in the playground watching their kids going into the classroom, Morag had to sit at home, alone. This says it all. Why oh why didn't the social workers realise the devastating effects that such a decision would have on a mother? It beggars belief.

If Jasmine had been allowed to contact her mum, that might have helped too. A telephone call from America every so often, or a card, or a letter. But nothing. She was under the Chapmans' control. Jasmine wasn't allowed to send anything to Scotland. She wasn't allowed to call her mum nor her grandmother. We sent lots of presents, but we got no response. Yet again, other people had acted against the needs of Morag and Jasmine. I thought Christians were supposed to "forgive"? To help and to assist are strong beliefs of Christians across the world. So why did the Chapmans, who profess to be people of faith, fail to acknowledge the deep hurt they were causing Morag?

With no help from the social workers, and with no contact from her child, it was little wonder that my heartbroken daughter was never able to recover. With her head in turmoil, her body soon joined in too. Her health deteriorated, cancer took hold, and the end was in sight.

Local people stop me in the street and ask me how Jasmine is getting on? How old is she now? I have to tell those folk that Jasmine doesn't contact me. She blamed me for Morag's and her own life going wrong.

And so, this book is for you, Jasmine. I hope one day, you will read the story of your early life. When you do, you will learn the truth about your mother. Forget what others have said, your mother was a remarkable woman. A woman who cared passionately for her little girl and who fought endlessly so that mother and daughter could be together. However, the forces against her were just too great.

But love prevailed.

I am convinced that, as Morag took her last breath, there would have been one thing on her mind. Jasmine Jamee Dodds.

Your mother was proud of you, and I sincerely hope that you can be proud of her too.